STAND TO...

E. Satikha Lem

5/2/08

STAND TO...

A Journey to Manhood

E. Franklin Evans

iUniverse, Inc.
New York Lincoln Shanghai

STAND TO ...
A Journey to Manhood

Copyright © 2008 by Elbert Franklin Evans

iUniverse books may be ordered through booksellers or by contacting:

iUniverse
2021 Pine Lake Road, Suite 100
Lincoln, NE 68512
www.iuniverse.com
1-800-Authors (1-800-288-4677)

Because of the dynamic nature of the Internet, any Web addresses or links contained in this book may have changed since publication and may no longer be valid.

The views expressed in this work are solely those of the author and do not necessarily reflect the views of the publisher, and the publisher hereby disclaims any responsibility for them.

Cover author photo credit: Jim Cawthorne, Camera 1, Columbus, GA.

ISBN: 978-0-595-45053-4 (pbk)
ISBN: 978-0-595-69931-5 (cloth)
ISBN: 978-0-595-89363-8 (ebk)

Printed in the United States of America

But at my back I always hear Time's winged chariot hurrying near.

—Andrew Marvell (1621–1678)

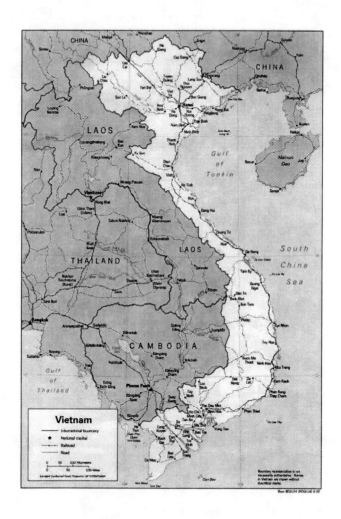

Contents

PROLOGUE 1

Chapter 1   LONGWOOD, FLORIDA 5

Chapter 2   CAM RAHN BAY 9

Chapter 3   ALPHA COMPANY 16

Chapter 4   NIGHT ON THE PERIMETER 24

Chapter 5   DUC LAP 28

Chapter 6   MOVE OUT 37

Chapter 7   CORDON AND SEARCH 53

Chapter 8   THE VOLCANO 62

Chapter 9   LANDING ZONE BASS 71

Chapter 10   RHADE VILLAGE 76

Chapter 11   CAMP ENARI 82

Chapter 12   PLEI TRAP VALLEY 87

Chapter 13   MAIL CALL 92

Chapter 14   LZ CHRISTMAS 97

Chapter 15   REST AND RECUPERATION 101

Chapter 16   THE PUNCHBOWL 105

Chapter 17   CHU PA MOUNTAIN 113

Chapter 18   LZ HIGHLANDER HEIGHTS 140

Chapter 19   TRI-BORDER 149

Chapter 20   CHANGE IN MISSION 156

Chapter 21   SPECIAL FORCES CAMP A-244 160

Chapter 22   BEN HET AND LOVIN' IT! 164

Chapter 23   INCOMING! 175

Chapter 24   SIEGE 180

Chapter 25   INFILTRATION 186

Chapter 26   ENEMY TANKS 191

Chapter 27   DOWNED PILOT 202

Chapter 28   ESCAPE PLANS 212

Chapter 29   MEDEVAC 218

Chapter 30   VISUAL RECON 222

Chapter 31   BACK TO THE WORLD 228

Chapter 32   STAND DOWN 233

Chapter 33   EPILOGUE 236

Chapter 34   BEN HET AT DUSK 239

GLOSSARY *243*

BIBLIOGRAPHY *259*

List of Illustrations

Alpha Company Leaders 124

Newly Commissioned Second Lieutenant of Infantry 125

Command Group 126

Poncho Hooch 127

Radio-Telephone Operator 128

Smoke Marks the Landing Zone 129

Loading onto Chinook, CH47 130

Author Sitting on a Bunker 131

Polei Kleng Waterhole 132

Bath Time at Polei Kleng 133

Platoon Sergeant Giving Candy to Montagnard
Children 134

Montagnard Children 135

Author Relaxing at Patrol Base 136

Author at Chu Pa Mountain 137

Damaged Russian Truck 138

New Home at LZ Highlander Heights 139

Ben Het Special Forces Camp 207

Damaged Russian PT76 Amphibious Tank 208

Tank Used by NVA in Attack 209

Destroyed NVA PT76 210

Photograph of PT 76 during recovery by Engineers 211

Ho Chi Minh Trail Marker 238

Villagers on Ben Het Trail 238

Montagnards Looking Back 241

ACKNOWLEDGEMENTS

I owe thanks to many people for encouraging me to write this book. The numerous nameless, though not insignificant, individuals I served alongside during my twenty-six years in the military have contributed greatly to this work, and I am very thankful for their influence. My sister, Barbara, whom I miss very much, departed from us suddenly. I value her strength and loving attitude. We were close, although most times geography separated us. My wife, who has been my love and most ardent critic, has made me into a better person than I would have been without her. Her courageous strength amazes me every day. My children, who bring me sunshine and joy as well as the challenges every parent experiences, make me feel young and very much loved and appreciated. My mother has encouraged me and expressed her pride in my small accomplishments. Because of her, I have attempted things that I never would have thought possible. My father's sacrifices that he made for his family and country gave me an inner strength and helped to shape my character. I must acknowledge the assistance rendered me by Mr. Robert "Deuce" Douglass and Mr. Robert Gross. Both published author-poets, they encouraged me and critiqued my work in progress. Thanks for letting me know that my story was worth the telling. Lastly, but extremely important to my writing efforts, is a special person who may not realize what she gave me. Dr. Virginia Spencer Carr was my English professor at Columbus College (now Columbus State University) in 1976. Her encouragement and guidance back then helped me to realize that I might possess some writing talent. Although it has taken me many years to try my skills, her influence has remained with me and helped nudge me to pursue my dream.

PROLOGUE

VIETNAM INTRODUCED ME to an early morning practice that recalled an abrupt awakening I'd had two years earlier as a teenage student. "Stand to" is short for "stand to arms." During World War I, it was believed that most enemy attacks occurred immediately before dawn. The practice of ensuring that all soldiers were awake and alert for an impending attack just before first light carried through into the Vietnam conflict. Each morning, soldiers on the defensive perimeters of firebases, patrol bases, and base camps were awakened and instructed to arm and dress in full combat gear. In World War I, stand to was also referred to as "the morning hate."

When I was nineteen, I experienced my own morning hate one Saturday morning. I've often thought of that terrible day and the aching feeling as I awakened to tragic news.

It has taken me over thirty-five years to begin writing this book. Although I've wanted to compose this book for many years, I didn't begin putting my thoughts on paper until July

2005. I always knew how my book would start, but the painful memory kept my words inside all these years. What finally prompted me to act? Perhaps it was accepting that I am mortal and that age is creeping up on me. Prior to this realization, the physical act of putting these words to paper was simply too painful. I wouldn't allow myself to think about the agonizing circumstances that led me to volunteer for Vietnam. My sister and I shared this pain since 1966, but neither of us would discuss that summer day when the war suddenly became personal for us. Over the years, I've wondered how my sister recalled that morning and how she coped with her grief. Fortunately, shortly before she died unexpectedly, we discussed our feelings about the incident. She told me it was comforting to know I was affected as strongly as she was, although neither of us could articulate those feelings for years.

That Saturday morning, I felt the private sorrow and anguish that many others had felt before me. That day was my awakening to world events outside my hometown. It was my "stand to," and now I had to look at the world a little differently. I had to prepare for whatever unpleasant, unexpected things might happen. Until then, the war was a televised broadcast of events somewhere far away. It didn't touch me except for a half hour each evening, after dinner, when I sat in front of the TV and watched curiously as Walter Cronkite summarized the day's combat events and casualties. It was an impersonal view and I was detached from the reality that these casualty numbers represented real people with families, friends, wives, and sweethearts. When it became heartbreaking, I put away the pain and tried not to think about it. Life went on and though I often thought about it, these thoughts were fleeting.

Many say that the healing process begins with an expression of sorrow. With this book, I began to express my sorrow for the first time in many years.

—July 18, 2007

1

LONGWOOD, FLORIDA

August 1966

"NOOOOOOOOOO. THEY'VE KILLLLLLED himmmmm!"

That primal scream stabbed into my sleepy unconsciousness like a cold ice pick. Instantly I knew that it was my younger sister's scream early that Saturday morning, yet I had never heard her voice filled with such agony and pain. Lying very still in my bed, I wanted to know what had caused that terrifying scream, although I dreaded the answer.

John Wayne had always been my hero, and I had watched every war movie he made several times. I was in awe as I watched him or Errol Flynn or Randolph Scott defeat the Nazis and Japs and lead their men through untold firefights and battles. War was exciting and heroes were made as they ruggedly fought and won each battle. Only when the hero died, like John

Wayne did in *The Sands of Iwo Jima*, did I feel saddened and a bit uncomfortable. But even when the hero died, it was only after he had conquered the enemy and left his men ready to carry on the fine tradition of eliminating their adversaries. Knowing I could watch my heroes' brave exploits in another movie, in another locale, in another war made it easier to bear when they died on screen.

When we lose a hero in real life, it isn't as easy.

Glenn had been my hero in high school even though he was only a couple of years older than me. He had been my surrogate older brother and one of my best friends during my last two years of high school. I had other buddies that I ran around with, but Glenn was the all-around good guy that I could talk with and not feel as if I had to pretend to be something I wasn't. Around Glenn I didn't always have to be trying to "make it" with some girl or prove how tough I was by drinking Southern Comfort and smoking Tampa Jewel cigars at all-night poker games. He was reserved and quiet but became animated when he talked about his love of history. He was especially interested in the Revolutionary War and the Civil War.

We often went camping in the woods behind our homes in the Florida swamps, where we could retreat from everyday boredom. Packing overnight bags, Glenn with a shotgun and me with a .22 caliber rifle, we were pioneers setting out to conquer the wilderness. I was the novice and Glenn was the experienced hunter. He knew the best camping sites and where to get clear water to drink when the Cokes ran out. In the woods, Glenn led and I followed.

Often while camping, we talked about what we planned to do with our lives. Glenn knew exactly what he wanted to do; he felt he was destined to be a soldier. In fact, sitting at our campfire one night, Glenn said he was sure he had been a soldier in a past life. He was positive he recalled parts of earlier battles from former times. He described the details of a particular private during the battle at Gettysburg—how he lived, what he ate, and the hardships he experienced marching through the rain and mud following the battle. He didn't share these thoughts with many others because of what they might think of him. He was particularly proud of the Civil War musket he owned. Once he let me shoot it, but usually he kept it close by his side or meticulously cleaned and well oiled at home.

As I quickly awakened that morning, I felt that something unspeakable had happened.

Glenn's sister walked down the street to inform us that Glenn had been killed in Vietnam a day earlier. My younger sister had begun dating Glenn shortly before he joined the army.

I walked into our living room to find my mother, her arms around my hysterical sister, tearfully thanking Glenn's sister for letting us know. I felt dizzy, as though in a dream. I thought, *Not Glenn. He can't be dead.*

It had only been a few months earlier when he was home that he was showing me the "rear takedown and stranglehold" he had learned in basic training. We practiced in his front yard to the amusement of our neighbors. No, Glenn had found his place in the world as a soldier and he couldn't be dead.

In stunned disbelief, I staggered up the street as I followed Glenn's sister home. Watching her enter their front door, I slowly walked across the front yard and reluctantly knocked on the door. After a few seconds, Glenn's father opened the door and I struggled to find the words even as they ached in my throat and the tears streamed down my face.

"Sir, if there's anything I can do …" I couldn't even finish the sentence.

Glenn's father knew. He said, "Son, there's nothing anyone can do now. Thank you." His grief was evident and I was suddenly embarrassed. All I could do was nod. As he shut the door, I slowly turned around and walked back home. A real hero had died.

I didn't know it then, but two years later, I would find myself in the jungles of Vietnam.

Several months after Glenn's death, his father stalled his car on a railroad crossing a few miles from home. Minutes later an oncoming train ended his life. No one knows for sure, but most felt that this was the way Glenn's father chose to cope with his personal grief.

2

CAM RAHN BAY

August 1968

"**L**ADIES AND GENTLEMEN, we are beginning our initial approach into Cam Rahn Bay, Republic of Vietnam. Please fasten your seatbelts."

An uneasy shuffle began throughout the cabin when the stewardess made the announcement. Everyone stretched, sat up, or moved so they could peer out the window at the country many of us had only seen on the evening news.

The government-contracted Continental Airlines flight had been long and tiring, with only short stopovers in Hawaii and Japan for refueling. Cards in our pockets declared we were members of the Imperial Order of the Golden Dragon, since we crossed the International Date Line hours ago. I recalled the feeling I had as we crossed that line; it represented a change in my life, as if I'd crossed the line into adulthood. However, my journey wasn't complete yet.

My past two years were filled with changes. A couple of semesters at Florida State after high school graduation showed me that I wasn't ready to focus on studies, so I tried working for Martin-Marietta, and even though the money was good for a nineteen-year-old, I felt an obligation to my buddy who had lost his life serving in that faraway country.

A few days before Thanksgiving, I signed my enlistment papers. I left for basic training in early December 1966. My father didn't want me to enlist in the army because he had served during World War II and still carried memories that haunted him. His brother, a glider pilot and my namesake, was killed in the Battle of the Bulge. Dad didn't talk about his own service in the Pacific, and he carried wounds inflicted by an enemy grenade that rendered him completely disabled in his later years. It wasn't until I completed Infantry Officer Candidate School that I began to feel he accepted my decision. I was surprised that his approval meant so much, because we weren't close as I grew up. My sister later told me how quiet Dad was the day I left. He watched my mother crying at the front door when I drove off a few days before I got on the plane for Southeast Asia.

Looking out the window as the aircraft descended, I was as anxious as he must have been when I told him I was leaving for Vietnam. He knew what jungle combat in the Pacific was like.

My daydreaming was interrupted by a pretty, young stewardess holding aerosol cans and spraying over our heads as she moved down the aisle. "Don't worry guys; this isn't harmful. It will only kill any insects we have on board."

"In that case, Smitty, you're done for," joked a nervous private.

"Bite me," fired back the Coke bottle-eyeglass wearing Smitty from across the aisle. The uneasy laughter relieved some of the tension.

"Ugly, isn't it?" asked the captain sitting in the seat on my right.

"Actually, sir, I think it looks pretty nice from up here."

"I don't mean the country. I mean Cam Rahn Bay. All that barbed wire, dust, and tin roofs."

"You're right. I was looking at the mountains and rice paddies."

"This your first trip across the ocean?" the captain asked.

The row of ribbons on his chest indicated he had been here before. "Yes, sir. Guess this is old hat to you."

"Well, I've been to Germany and this is my second trip to Vietnam. I'm planning to get back to my old outfit, the Fourth Engineers."

It was mid-morning at Cam Rahn Bay as the ground came into focus. A tropical postcard view of tiny green islands scattered along the irregular coastline reminded me of Oahu. As the plane flew inland, the puffy white clouds and brilliant blue sky were reflected in the stagnant water of the geometrically arranged patchwork quilt of rice paddies below. In the distance, undulating mountain peaks silhouetted against the horizon beckoned.

The ground came closer and I saw a long runway ahead. The large logistical facility was an ugly mark on the landscape. Barbed wire, metal planking, and squat huts filled the polluted scene. Fuel storage tanks were lined up in groups alongside the asphalt roads. Surrounding the strip were sandbagged bunkers manned by Vietnamese soldiers cradling M16 rifles. Armored personnel carriers (APCs) equipped with heavy-caliber machine guns were scattered around the edge of the runway. Interspersed around the APCs I saw several dusters. These deadly self-propelled armored weapon systems, outfitted with 40mm automatic cannons, were designed for antiaircraft defense, but their rapid rate of fire also made them extremely effective against ground attacks.

As the plane touched down, the cabin became silent. I prepared to disembark as the other passengers began to stand, stretch, and reach for their bags. After receiving a short briefing on the plane, we were directed to buses that carried us on to the in-processing center. Except for the windshield, all the windows on the buses were covered by steel mesh wire. The captain I had sat next to on the plane explained, "The purpose of the mesh is to prevent grenades from being tossed in through the windows. Welcome to Vietnam."

At the in-processing center, we were divided into groups according to rank and began filing out the stacks of paperwork, turning in our personnel and medical records. Our greenbacks were exchanged for Vietnamese currency and Military Payment Certificates (or MPC). We were not allowed to use US currency in country.

Several hours later, we were again loaded onto buses and taken to our temporary quarters. Most were exhausted from the long ride on the aircraft and collapsed onto their bunks for the remainder of the night. Next morning I arose to the smells of bacon and coffee. It was raining heavily outside, and I carefully walked on the planks between the tents while trying to keep out of the mud as much as possible. Our meal of scrambled eggs, potatoes, bacon, soggy toast, orange juice, and coffee tasted wonderful. The milk was the same reconstituted powdered milk that I recalled from my childhood in West Virginia. It still tasted terrible.

That morning we were given our initial unit assignments and told that transportation would be available for those of us going to the Fourth Infantry Division after lunch. Later that day we loaded onto a C-130 aircraft for the short flight to Pleiku, squeezing into the nylon web seats that lined the bulkheads. The flight was loud since there was no insulation on the interior of the plane. Upon arrival at the Pleiku airport, we transferred to buses again for the ride through the city to Camp Enari, the division base camp.

The next three days went by quickly as we in-processed and received briefings on the customs and traditions of the Vietnamese people and the various ethnic groups of the central highlands.

The second day, at Enari, we were given a quick orientation on the terrain, including an instinctive firing course incorporating typical Việt Cộng fighting positions, bunkers, spider holes, and camouflage techniques. During breaks from the schedule, Montagnard women and children sold bottled colas and souvenirs. Although I had read a little about them in the booklet provided us upon arrival to the division, this was my first opportunity to see these ethnic mountain people up close. Various tribes inhabited the highlands and lived pretty much the same way they had for centuries, as hunters and gatherers. These simple people and the Vietnamese shared an intense mutual dislike.

Montagnard loyalties were limited to their villages and elders. They distrusted both the Vietnamese government and the Việt Cộng. Unfortunately for them, they were often caught in the middle of the two groups as each attempted to exploit them. They were often conscripted into service for one side or the other with predictable grievous results.

As I observed these indigenous inhabitants, I bought a small bottled Coke from a shriveled, toothless old woman who carried a hand-woven basket of colas on one arm and a larger woven basket filled with wooden crafts on the other. I estimated her age to be around fifty. Nearby, laid out on a blanket, she had handmade crossbows for sale. I paid her a few Vietnamese piasters for my cool drink; she grinned and removed a pungent hand-rolled cigar from her mouth. I recognized the odor of marijuana as she reached over her shoulder and passed the cigar to a baby that I hadn't noticed. The baby was strapped to her back with a cloth wrap. I watched in astonishment as the baby took the cigar and calmly placed it in its mouth as though it were the most normal pacifier in the world. I realized that she must be the mother of this child. Her age was probably closer to thirty than fifty but the hardships of her lifestyle showed in each wrinkle of her leathery skin. Before I left, I found her and bought one of her long hand-carved wooden pipes. It was trimmed in brass with a large bowl at one end shaped like a bird. She had retrieved her cigar from the baby. While puffing on it, she took my money once again, still smiling broadly with her toothless grin.

Upon return to the second brigade's rear command post at Camp Enari, we were told to report to the S1 or personnel officer. Looking us over seriously, Captain Thurston, the S1, asked, "Anyone have mechanized experience?"

The only experience I had with armored personnel carriers was in OCS at Benning, and I recalled that I didn't like all the maintenance that each troop carrier required. I remained quiet as one of the other lieutenants spoke up.

"I spent some time in a mech unit before OCS, Captain," said a muscular first lieutenant.

"OK, then you're assigned to the second of the eighth mechanized battalion."

"Evans, you and Warden go with the first of the Twelfth. All of you be here at the headquarters and be prepared to move out at 0730 tomorrow. You'll need to go to supply and draw your weapons right after breakfast. Your ammo and web gear will be issued then, too."

Arising early the following morning, we ate breakfast and picked up our gear from the supply room. I was handed an M16 and four empty magazines. I began to feel as if I was in a war zone.

"You'll get your ammunition and grenades when you arrive at your unit," the supply sergeant said. "Your transportation to the helipad is right outside." He pointed to a row of vehicles lined up on the gravel and mud road.

After saying quick good-byes to my new friends who were going to other units, I climbed aboard the waiting deuce-and-a-half truck from the First Battalion of the Twelfth Infantry Regiment and headed off to the helicopter for the next leg of my journey.

3
ALPHA COMPANY

August 1968

LOOKING OVER THE treetops as the Huey approached Alpha Company's location, I saw a small clearing in the trees appear on the left side of the chopper. Strewn about the bare spot was a perimeter of fifteen or so sandbagged bunkers with one or two makeshift poncho tents immediately behind each. Roughly in the center of the circle was a larger bunker, two poncho hootches, and a small fire with a couple of men cooking their dinner. Yellow smoke from a smoke grenade was drifting off to the south from the landing zone just outside the perimeter. Expertly, the pilot scooted above the treetops and landed in the LZ. Second Lieutenant Mike Warden and I quickly jumped off the chopper and walked toward the nearest individual standing nearby. As we got closer, I noticed he had captain's bars pinned to his helmet. *This must be the company commander*, I thought.

Mike and I saluted at the same time. "Sir, Lieutenant Evans reports," I said loudly. "Lieutenant Warden here, sir," Mike said a bit more casually.

"OK, Lieutenants," he said, snapping a quick salute back. "I'm Captain Dick Trotter. Warden, you go see that Captain standing over there," he said pointing to a nearby officer. "Evans, come with me."

I followed Captain Trotter to his company command post, or CP, where he introduced me to First Sergeant MacCardle.

"Toss your gear over there for the time being," Captain Trotter said, indicating a spot nearby. He reached for a large can of boiling water on the small fire, poured some into his C-ration coffee cup, and stirred in the coffee. "Sit down and relax for a few minutes."

Captain Trotter lit a cigarette. "By the way, skip the saluting here in the bush. It seems to attract bullets." Squatting next to the fire he said, "What'd you do before coming to Vietnam?"

"I was at Fort Benning, sir. Graduated from OCS last November, assigned to the Ranger Department for a while, then volunteered for duty here."

"What did you do with the Rangers?"

"I taught counter-guerilla patrolling. You know, ambushes, raids, quick-kill techniques. Was mainly working with OCS and Basic Officer students. Occasionally, I taught the NCOC students. You know, the instant NCO course."

"Oh, yeah, the 'shake and bake' course. We've got a few of your graduates here. That's good. I need a platoon leader for Third Platoon."

Off to the west I heard several small explosions. They sounded one or two kilometers away. I looked in that direction.

"That's where we spent last night. Charlie is dropping 82mm mortar rounds where he thinks we are. We humped here early this morning. Unfortunately, by tonight he'll probably figure out where we are now. Supply birds have been in and out all day long. We'll be in this patrol base one more day, then chopper to Ban Me Thout—here on the map." He pointed to our location and then, pointing to another, said, "Here's where we were last night. As you can see, it's about two clicks to the west."

Pointing once again, he said, "Four days ago in this area we made contact with a company of dinks and lost a couple of our men in Third Platoon. Lieutenant Wood wasn't much help. Third Platoon was on point, up front when Charlie opened up with AK fire. Instead of leading his platoon, Wood was banging his CAR 15 against a tree trying to break the rusted bolt free." Trotter shook his head. "Now his men don't trust him." The lines around his mouth hardened as he said, "Neither do I. Fortunately he has a good platoon sergeant, Sergeant Clyde Chapel."

I listened closely as Trotter explained the company's mission and said that we would be moving to a new location soon. He was waiting for the battalion to send the order. In the meantime, we would stay here for a day or so.

"There's a North Vietnamese regiment operating around Ban Me Thout. Our battalion's gonna try to find them. The local Việt Cộng are operating in strengths of eighty-to one-hundred-man company-sized units. The leadership cadre move into the villages at night to hold their political meetings and recruit replacements—voluntarily or forcefully."

He paused, "Since you're new here, watch Sergeant Chapel. Around the villages you've got to watch out for punji stakes and other booby traps near the trails. Nasty things those punji stakes. Sharpened bamboo stakes hidden in the tall grass. Sometimes they're camouflaged in a hole right on the trail or buried in pits along the sides. The Kit Carson scouts have pointed several out so far."

I recalled what my friend Glenn had told me two years earlier about these sharpened bamboo sticks with human feces smeared on them. "Yeah, I've heard about the punji stakes, but what are Kit Carson scouts?"

"They're former VC soldiers who surrendered and agreed to work for our side. Mainly they assist with interrogating prisoners and talking to the local villagers. They're also pretty savvy in spotting the enemy. The Vietnamese term for them is Chieu Hoi, or Open Arms. We've got three of them with us. They're with Third Platoon."

Former bad guys working with us? I thought. That did nothing to calm my nerves.

Trotter stood, shook the few remaining drops of his coffee over the fire, and said, "You ready to go?"

Speaking with more confidence than I felt, I nodded and said, "Yes, sir."

I hefted my rucksack on my back, grabbed my M16, and followed Captain Trotter. We walked across the clearing, stopping at a poncho hooch several yards inside the perimeter. A pair of boots stuck out of the tent, and Trotter kicked them.

"Lieutenant Wood, grab your shit. You're relieved. Lieutenant Evans is here to replace you."

Wood crawled out of the tent; he seemed to move in slow motion, lifeless. He picked up his gear and weapon, looked at

Trotter, and turned to me, "I've been expecting you. Here, do you want my carbine? It's a lot lighter than your M16."

I gave it a fleeting look and said, "No, thanks. I'll keep my M16."

Wood shrugged. "OK. I left my ammo, grenades, and extra chow in the hooch. Help yourself."

Captain Trotter said, "Wood, the supply chopper's inbound. You catch it on the way out. See the battalion S1 at the battalion CP. He'll give you directions there."

"Yes, sir. So long."

With shoulders sagging Wood walked away without turning back, and Trotter shook his head in disgust. Turning to me and nodding towards the individual who had walked up to us, he said, "This is your platoon sergeant, Sergeant Chapel. Listen to him."

Without another word, Trotter strode off towards his CP.

I could read Platoon Sergeant Clyde Chapel's thoughts as he reached out his hand. *Great. Another dumb lieutenant to break in.*

"Well, Lieutenant, you are now the platoon leader of Third Platoon, Alpha Company, First Battalion, Twelfth Infantry. Throw your gear over there next to the hooch."

"Thanks, Sergeant." I set my rucksack and other gear next to the hooch where LT Wood had been. I took a pack of cigarettes out of my pocket and offered one to Sergeant Chapel, then lit one for myself. "Captain Trotter says you've been here awhile."

Looking distastefully at the cigarette, Sergeant Chapel tore off the filter, tossed it on the ground, and stuck the butt in his mouth. He lit the cigarette and took a deep drag. Exhaling slowly, he said, "Yes, sir. I'm going home in a few weeks."

"Well, look, while you're here I'm going to need your help. I'd appreciate it if you'd let me know if you think I'm doing something stupid. I know I'm green, but I'm a quick study. I'll have to rely on your experience."

"As long as we work together and keep our heads, we'll do OK." He sat down, took a drink of coffee, and said, "Lieutenant Wood was lucky. He didn't belong in the bush leading soldiers. I'm surprised he lasted this long."

"What happened?"

"We were the lead platoon for the company and our point came under fire from a couple of dinks with automatic weapons. Jones and Martinez hit the ground, returned fire, and called back for help. I sent a machine gunner up front to help take the pressure off the point. We returned fire and the VC started hitting us from two directions. After exchanging fire, the CO got on the radio and called for air support. He got a forward air controller on the radio and coordinated for close air support."

"That must've upset Charlie's day."

"Well, it should have, except our support came from Vietnamese Air Force or VNAF Skyraiders. Vietnamese pilots. Somehow in the radio traffic there was a mix-up in our exact location and the pilots strafed the company. We popped red smoke to designate our positions and the pilots were told the enemy was a hundred meters to the front of our smoke. Not sure if Charlie popped red smoke too, but the cannon fire raked our platoon. We lost one killed and two wounded. Should have never used the VNAF for close in support, but that's all that was available. During this whole time, Wood was about thirty meters behind the point banging his weapon against a tree trying to get it to function." Nodding in the direction of my weapon, he said, "I heard Lieutenant Wood offer you his carbine. Good call keeping your M16."

"Yeah, Captain Trotter told me about Wood's rusted weapon. How's the platoon doing? Any problems?"

"No, they're all right, except during the firefight, Wilkes, the machine gunner, panicked and ran to the rear taking his gun with him. Good kid, but some of the men feel they can't count on him anymore. He'll be OK. Come on, let's walk the platoon area and I'll introduce you to the squad leaders."

We walked around our platoon's portion of the perimeter and talked with each man. "Over there are the Kit Carson scouts. Did the captain tell you about them?"

"Yeah. How long have they been with you?"

"Two days. They are going to work with us for a couple of weeks, I think. I'm not real sure about them, but so far they're OK. All former VC. The Việt Cộng and the NVA would kill them immediately if they were captured, so they have a real incentive to work closely with us. That taller skinny one we call Abbott. The short one's Costello. The older one, Huong, speaks a little English and some French, too. He was a former sergeant."

The two younger VC scouts looked to be in their late teens or early twenties. Huong was probably in his late twenties. They all had dark, leathery skin and looked as if they had been outdoors all their lives. They wore tiger stripe fatigues. They were armed with M1 carbines and Huong had a US Army M14. That made me a bit uneasy. I decided to keep a close watch on them. I nodded in their direction. Abbott and Costello laughed and began talking rapidly among themselves. I guessed my inexperience showed. Even though they were young, these guys were already seasoned combat veterans.

During our walk around the defensive positions, I noticed that razor-sharp concertina wire and strands of barbed wire tanglefoot encircled the perimeter. I could also see several claymore mines and trip flares near the outer edge of the wire obstacles. In front of each bunker, the brush had been thinned in order to provide clear fields of fire to limit any attacker's cover and concealment. The M60 machineguns were positioned to cover the flat open spaces. The machinegun's grazing fire during an attack could be devastating eighteen to thirty-six inches above the ground.

"We have two observation posts about seventy-five meters out to our platoon's front. At night, we'll put listening posts in closer. Let's go get some hot chow," said Chapel. "Soon it'll be time to bring in the OPs and send out the LPs."

4
NIGHT ON THE PERIMETER

August 1968

T HE LAST GLIMMER of light crowned the distant trees and slowly faded to blackness. I sat on a sandbagged bunker drinking a cup of hot chocolate. I looked up at the stars and listened to the sounds from the jungle, unusual but somehow soothing. They reminded me of the sounds in the Florida swamps near Big Tree Park. Even the smells of the jungle were familiar, reminding me of peaceful nights camping a few miles from home.

A few yards to my right, my third squad leader, Staff Sergeant Baker, was giving final instructions to two of his men before they moved out to their listening post. He spoke quietly. "All right, you guys, I want you to maintain complete silence while you're out there. Only use your radio to send your hourly SITREPS. Use your push-to-talk switch to break squelch. Once for 'yes' or 'everything's OK.' Squeeze the switch twice for 'negative' or 'we've got movement.' Got it?"

"Yeah, Sarge. We know," replied one of the men.

"Well, this is Brown's first time on LP, so I want to make sure you all got it right."

"Don't worry 'bout me, Sarge. I got it," said PFC Brown.

"OK. Move out and be quiet moving into your position. Let me know when you're all set. Keep your ears alert for Charlie. We know the VC are moving through this area at night."

The LPs quietly moved into their night locations using the designated paths through the protective wire defenses. Should they have to return quickly, they would use these same routes to run back to the safety of the perimeter. Upon arriving in their night positions they radioed back and maintained silence. Hourly situation reports, or SITREPS, would be relayed to the platoon CP through the prearranged radio signals. No voice communications would be sent unless enemy movement was detected. Earlier in the day the company's 81mm mortars had registered defensive fires. Our supporting 105mm artillery battery was prepared to provide indirect fire support if necessary. These fires would help cover the quick return of the LPs.

I sipped my cocoa and tried to spot any movement in the blackness in the jungle in front of me. Ahead in the darkness, I heard the sound of the "re-up" bird. "Ree-uup, ree-uup" was its high-pitched trill. Re-up was the army slogan for "reenlist." Re-up for four more years was the cry of the battalion reenlistment NCO. More often than not, the answer from the soldier was an impolite version of "No way, Sarge." Tonight, a jungle lizard answered the bird with a staccato "Fuck you. Fuck you." I heard the snickers from the soldiers on the bunker on my left. They enjoyed this jungle sonata, which echoed their own sentiments.

Re-up? Fuck you. You found humor in unlikely places in the bush, and this small bit of humor was peculiarly calming.

Next to me, on the top of the bunker, the squad leader had arranged his ammunition, grenades, radio, and protective gas mask. In the dark, he would know exactly where the needed supplies were located so he wouldn't have to fumble or search for them in the darkness. The firing devices for the claymore mines were also in pre-selected spots for quick retrieval. I could hear the men of the platoon beginning to settle into the routine for the evening. Each bunker would have at least one sentry, and throughout the night every man would, in turn, pull his share of night watch. Sergeant Chapel and I would take turns checking the bunkers to ensure that the sentries remained awake. Each squad leader maintained contact with the LPs to his front and reported their status to my radio operator hourly.

"Quiet tonight, Lieutenant," said Sergeant Chapel as he perched next to me on the bunker.

"Yeah. Just hope it remains quiet."

"The CO just sent a runner to the CP. He has a mission for us tomorrow. Looks like we'll be leaving this patrol base in the afternoon. He wants to see all the platoon leaders in the morning at 0715."

"OK. Where are we headed?"

"Somewhere called Duc Lap."

"OK. Well, the LPs are in position now and I'm ready to settle in for the night. How about you? Which shift do you want?"

"I'm not tired, so I guess I'll take the first one."

"In that case, I'm heading to the hooch for a few hours of sleep. Wake me when it's my turn."

"WILCO, sir."

As Sergeant Chapel departed in one direction and I in another, I heard a soft "Ree-uup. Ree-uup." To my left, in the vicinity of the second squad, I also heard a softer "Fuck you. Fuck you." Lizard or bird? Or soldier? Who knows? In the blackness they all sounded alike.

5

DUC LAP

August 1968

D UC LAP AIRSTRIP sat at the base of a hill. The SF's Civilian Irregular Defense Group (CIDG) camp was perched on top. Surrounded by NVA infantry less than a week ago, the camp still showed signs of the intense battle. During the battle, the NVA had overrun the small northern portion of the hill. Reinforcing mobile strike force units of Nung mercenaries prevented Duc Lap's total annihilation. Failing to overrun the whole camp, the NVA had retreated across the border temporarily to regroup and care for their casualties. Our battalion, designated Task Force Spoiler, was ordered to Duc Lap to protect the airstrip and camp.

Offloading the CH47s that brought us here, I gave the order to Third Platoon to spread out and take up temporary positions. Our mission was to protect the camp and prevent the NVA from coming back across the border in strength.

Captain Trotter's voice came over the radio. "One-Six, Two-Six, Three-Six. This is Six-One."

The other platoons answered in turn. "This is Three-Six," I replied.

"Keep your troops' heads down. We're going to register arty in fifteen mikes. Over." In fifteen minutes, 105mm artillery rounds would be impacting nearby to establish DEFCONS, or defensive concentrations, in the event we needed indirect fire support during the night.

"This is Three-Six. WILCO. Over." The other platoon leaders again responded.

"Will report end of mission. Out."

I passed the word to my squad leaders and found a comfortable position to sit out the loud impact of the rounds.

"Sir, how long do you think we'll be here?" asked Mac, my radio-telephone operator (RTO).

"Don't know. The CO said we need to secure the area while the CIDG repair damages to the camp. I understand they took a good beating. Five Special Forces troops were killed and the NVA occupied the top briefly. Tomorrow we move out to higher ground. I should be getting the company commander's order shortly."

The deafening impact of an artillery round shook the ground. Instinctively, I tightened my body into a small ball.

"Man that was close," Mac yelled.

Another impact shook the ground and was immediately followed by buzzing, whirring sounds as bits of metal flew through the air. The buzzing ended with a loud thump. Dead shrapnel. More artillery rounds impacted, sending shards of metal through the air. These jagged pieces of metal then deflected off objects, spinning through the air once again. Although they lost most of their initial force and probably weren't lethal anymore, they could still cause serious injury. Those friendly artillery rounds were hitting mighty close.

WHAM! Buzzzz … SMACK!

"Damnation!" I yelled. I felt a sharp sting in the small of my back as a small piece of metal slapped into me.

"You OK, sir?"

"Yeah. That smarts though." I felt my back. It was burning and tender. "Give me the radio handset. I'll tell the CO to call it off. It's getting too close and someone's going to get hurt." Mac pushed the handset into my outstretched hand.

Immediately another artillery round struck the ground nearby. It was followed by three more in rapid succession. Once again, the whirring sounds signaled the metal pieces flying around us. I curled up as they slammed against the ground. A close one ended with another loud smack.

"Shit! Damn it … damn it to hell," Mac yelled, rolling over on his back pulling the radio handset out of my grasp.

"Mac, are you OK?" I yelled.

"I think so, but it hit me right in the cheek of my ass." He shucked out of his rucksack and radio harness and rubbed his rear. He felt around on the ground. "Here … look at this."

"Six-One, this is Three-Six. Call off the arty. We've got metal flying all over the place."

"Roger, Three-Six. Ceasefire in effect."

I looked at the piece of metal that Mac was now holding. It was about the size of a pocketknife and had jagged edges. Fortunately, that one didn't have enough force left to pierce the skin, but it must have hurt like hell.

"Well, sir. I guess if this had been enemy mortars I would have qualified for a Purple Heart, right?"

I knew that he was in a little pain. I was, too. Still, I couldn't help but laugh at our predicament. Trying hard not to laugh, I said, "I guess so. Good for you it didn't hit you in the head. I would have had to replace you."

"Guess I'll keep this souvenir since I don't get a Purple Heart. Just have to settle for a large welt and a purple bruise."

"We could invent a new award: a Purple Ass."

"Thanks, sir," Mac said sarcastically.

"Check with the squads to see if anyone else got hit."

Fortunately, only one other soldier was hit and he took it in the helmet. It tore a small rip in the camouflage cover thanks to his steel pot.

My platoon medic put some salve and a small bandage on my cut and looked at Mac's posterior. "You'll live, Mac. Won't even have a scar. It'll be tender for a day or so, and you'll have a nice big bruise for about a week."

"Great," Mac muttered. "Purple Ass. It's not funny."

◆　　　◆　　　◆

OK, gents. That's it," said Captain Trotter as he completed his orders on the upcoming mission. "We'll cordon and search the hamlet at first light tomorrow. Prepare to combat assault at 1600 today enroute to our new night location. Tomorrow morning, early, we hump to the hamlet about three clicks away. Any questions?"

"Sir, what about the Kit Carson Scouts?" asked Sergeant Singleton. "What's their job on this mission?"

"Good question, Sergeant. I didn't cover them yet. Their job is to lead us into position before light and then talk with the villagers to get whatever info they can. Also, they'll interrogate any prisoners we take. They'll work with the five-man team from the National Police, who will join us after we secure the hamlet. Anything else?"

No one had any questions, so we moved back to our CPs to prepare our orders for the squad leaders. I was mentally going over the order format so my first combat order to my men would be correct. I wanted this order to be letter perfect. Time to show my stuff.

Sergeant Singleton gathered the squad leaders at the CP, where I issued the verbal order in the format I had learned so well in OCS. In detail, I laid out the plan for our platoon from the combat assault by helicopter to moving into our designated portion of the cordon encircling the hamlet. Each squad had a role and order of movement throughout the mission. The 81mm mortar platoon would provide close in fire support, if needed, and the search team, second squad, would search our piece of the hamlet. I noticed the Kit Carson Scouts watching me with bemused expressions. I doubted they understood.

"OK, men. Go brief your squads and get ready to chopper out beginning at 1300 hours. Any questions?" There were none, so I felt I did a pretty decent job giving my first combat order. As the squad leaders walked back to their squad locations, I turned to Sergeant Singleton. "Well, Sergeant Singleton, did I forget anything?"

"No, sir. That was just about the best damned schoolbook order I ever heard. All five paragraphs without missing a step."

Detecting a bit of sarcasm, I said, "All right. Give it to me. How did I do?"

"Well, sir. You did great for your first order, but here we don't need a detailed order. A short FRAGO will work just fine. These guys have been together for several months. They're used to working together and know most of the routine by heart. You'll get the hang of it after a couple of times."

I said, "Thanks for bursting my bubble."

"No sweat, sir. Glad to do it." Smiling, he said, "We'll rub some of that green off you soon enough."

"Thanks. I think I'll clean up now. Maybe some of that green will wash off."

Before I cleaned up, I decided to write a quick letter to my wife. We had been married about three and a half months and I missed her terribly. I had promised her I would never remove my new wedding band, and as I rolled it around my finger I thought of her. I carried a picture of her taken only a few days before I left. I took it out of my pocket to look at. She wore leopard spotted pajamas with my black Ranger beret, and her short, dark hair framed her face.

"You wife, Thiu Úy?" Huong, the scout, had walked up quietly and startled me.

"Yes … yes, it is." I held the picture so he could see it better.

"She very pretty. She Vietnamese?"

"No. She's American." I could see why Huong thought she might be Vietnamese. Her olive skin, dark hair, and military-style pajamas did make her look Oriental. I hadn't thought of that before the scout mentioned it.

"Oh, pretty wife. You miss very much, I bet."

Rubbing my ring, I said, "Yes, I do."

"My wife dead. Daughter and son with sister."

"I'm sorry."

"Me, too." He quietly walked away and joined the other scouts. I understood how he must have felt losing his wife and now working with these strange Americans, who stayed for a while and then went back home to their loved ones. His only hope of rejoining his family was the end of this war. If he survived it. The odds of that were not good since he was in it for the duration, however long it lasted.

I pocketed the picture and sat down to write my letter. I was homesick for the first time since arriving. Tomorrow was my first combat mission and I wanted to get this letter off before then.

I finished the letter and put it in the sandbag marked mail for pickup by the resupply chopper. I picked up my versatile steel pot helmet and filled it with warm water from the canteen cup that had been warming over the breakfast fire. Using my towel and a small bar of soap, I washed my face and hands, then lathered up for a shave. Not much to shave, but I thought it would make me feel better. I quickly shaved, then toweled off and dried my hands. Picking up my makeshift washbasin, I tossed the water from my helmet into the bushes.

Oh, crap! I noticed that my wedding ring wasn't on my finger. It must have come off in the warm, soapy water in my steel pot. Near panic gripped me. *I can't lose that ring. It wasn't ever supposed to come off my finger. Got to find it.*

I got down on my knees and searched every inch of the bushes where I had thrown my soapy water. That ring was nowhere around. How could I tell my wife? My carelessness had cost me the one symbol that physically linked me with home. I felt a sense of dread, as if this might be an omen. I had to find my ring. No luck. After fifteen minutes of searching, I finally realized I was never going to find it. I walked over to my hooch, squatted next to my ruck, and lit a cigarette.

I decided to write another letter. However painful it would be, I had to explain to my wife that I had lost my wedding band and ask her to buy a replacement to send to me immediately. Although it wouldn't be the same, it would have to do. As I began to write, a shadow fell upon the letter.

"You lose?"

I looked up to find Huong smiling and holding out a gleaming gold wedding band.

"I sure did." I smiled and leaped up. Huong had seen me searching for something in the bushes and, after I gave up, began a thorough search that turned up the missing ring. I held out my hand. He dropped it into my palm as I grinned broadly. I didn't know whether to shake his hand or hug him. I decided a handshake would be best.

"Pretty wife now happy," he said as he turned to walk away.

"Huong, wait." I called after him. "Thank you very, very much."

"No sweat," he said, grinning.

What could I give him for his kindness? I reached down to my web gear and unfastened my shiny new KA-BAR knife and sheath. I had purchased them at Ranger Joe's a few days before I left for Vietnam.

"This is for you. Thank you again."

"No. You keep. May need." He paused. "You got cigarette?"

"Of course. Here, take the whole pack." As he took my nearly full pack of Winston's, I reached into my pocket, took out my Zippo lighter, and offered to light his cigarette. As Huong saw the lighter, with the Infantry School's "Follow Me" symbol engraved on one side, he smiled widely and looked at me with a quizzical expression. It was obvious that he considered this a worthy prize.

"Please take this with my thanks."

"OK. Can do." He quickly reached for the lighter. Taking it, he lit his cigarette, flicked the lighter a few times, and walked back to his friends smiling.

I felt much better. I tore up the unfinished letter and tossed it into the fire. Absentmindedly, I reached into my empty pocket for a cigarette. Finding none, I smiled. *Oh, yeah*, I thought. Then I sat down, leaned back against a tree stump, closed my eyes, and breathed contentedly.

6

MOVE OUT

September 1968

I T WAS QUIET throughout the night. The next day we got the order to move to a patrol base five clicks away. Departing around 1300, we planned to be in our night position before dark. The next several days would be filled with sending out local patrols and ambushes to detect VC or NVA moving back into the area.

"Saddle up! Time to move out." I ordered. "First Squad leads out. I'll be right behind you."

We moved down the trail while constantly watching our left and right flanks. As I looked ahead, I saw Huong pick something off the bushes along the side of the trail and put it in his mouth. He was eating something and began putting more in his shirt pocket. The other scouts did the same. I looked down to my right and noticed small red peppers growing on some of the bushes. Good. I liked hot peppers, too. This was just like picking blackberries while training back at Benning. Cautiously I picked one and bit the tip off the end.

Holy crap! I had just bit into a white-hot molten bar of iron. Nothing that small could burn so badly. I sputtered, spat, and grabbed for my canteen. Pouring water all over my mouth and swishing it around inside provided me no relief. If Charlie had been anywhere in the immediate area, he would have heard my cursing and spitting for at least fifty meters. Mac roared with laughter. So did everyone in sight as they watched me dance around in pain.

I heard Captain Trotter's voice on the radio. "Three-Six, this is Six-One. What's the commotion up front?"

I couldn't breathe, let alone talk. My lips were burning and my tongue was on fire. I motioned for Mac to talk to the CO for me.

"Six-One, this is Three-Six Alpha. Three-Six can't talk right now. He's too busy spitting out hot peppers." Mac was laughing so hard that he could hardly get the words out. "He might not be able to talk until tomorrow. Over."

Mac listened to the radio for a moment, then said, "Roger, out." Turning to me he said, "Sir, the old man says 'OK. Eat some crackers, but move out.'"

I took a candy bar out of my pocket hoping it would help lessen the fire. I took a large bite and motioned for the patrol to move out. After a while, the pain did lessen a bit and I could talk, although the burning continued for more than hour. Huong and the other scouts continued to pick and eat the peppers as we moved through the jungle.

For the next hour we walked, keeping our eyes open for any movement ahead of us. The point element was alert for booby traps and the scouts moved with them. Soon the point squad radioed back that we had to cross a rice paddy or detour to the right, which would add another two thousand meters. Since we had to be in our night position before dark, I gave the order to keep moving ahead but to spread out to twice the normal interval between men. It was slow moving in the waist high rice paddy. The monsoon rains had filled the paddies and the rice was already growing a foot or more above the waterline.

"Three-Six, this is one-one Bravo. Over," the point radioed.

"Three-Six. Over."

"We have a small hooch in the center of the rice paddy. Appears to be unoccupied. Over."

"Roger. Approach it carefully and check it out."

"WILCO."

Five minutes later the call came over the radio again, "Three-Six. This is One-One Bravo. The hooch is empty. No sign of anyone around. Over."

"Roger, One-One Bravo. Keep moving. Look out for booby traps. Out."

Another hour passed and the point element radioed that they had arrived at the designated night location. They reported the ruins of a building in the center of a clearing. I walked into the clearing and saw the destroyed remains of a former French colonial home that dominated the site. Built of concrete and stone, it wasn't a large building, but its solid construction reflected the aspirations of the builders for permanency. The roof was gone and fire and explosions had destroyed two of the walls. The remaining two walls were pockmarked with bullet holes. I could tell that once it had been a comfortable home built with a high ceiling, several rooms, and many narrow windows. It was probably home to the French planter who managed the small rubber plantation there. I imagined that here the family of the planter had lived a happy, contented life until, sometime in the not too distant past, the war had forced the inhabitants to abandon it.

Seventy-five meters to the south of the structure was a clearing with several grass-covered bumps rising three to four feet above the ground. Graves, possibly all of the inhabitants hadn't left and the past residents were buried there. Whomever these graves held, their untold stories were lost in the day-to-day struggles of the forces that seesawed back and forth through the area

We moved into the location without incident and began setting up the perimeter for the night. OPs were posted for security. Other soldiers began to dig their three-man bunkers, sight in their claymore mines, and clear brush to allow better fields of fire. Machineguns were given positions that could best provide covering fire and protective barbed wire was placed forward of the bunkers. Finally, I sat down to heat my evening meal of C-rations, ham slices, cooked over a C-4 fire. Opening the can with my P-38 opener, I prepared to add cheese.

"Thiu Úy. You come. Eat with us." Huong stood smiling next to me. "Bring food." He pointed to my cans.

Earlier I had seen the scouts preparing their meals in a large pot over an open fire. I watched as they boiled water and then added rice, the small fiery-hot red peppers they had harvested on the trail, and some other leaves and roots that I didn't recognize. I reached for my canteen, weapon, and cigarettes. Why not? It would be a welcomed change from the repetitive C-ration fare.

"Sure," I said, getting to my feet. "Thanks."

We walked over to the fire and I squatted down next to Huong. I offered my can of ham slices and an unopened can of cheese. Huong took both and emptied the contents into the boiling pot. He also threw a handful of bamboo shoots and bean sprouts into the mix. Then he emptied a small bottle of Tabasco sauce into the pot. Oh, boy, this was going to be a flavorful stew. I hoped I brought enough water. Huong offered me a freshly carved set of chopsticks and showed me how to use them. In my pocket was a plastic spoon.

It was delicious—spicy but not flaming hot. I was surprised, remembering my earlier experience with the small red peppers. Apparently, cooking them and adding other ingredients subdued the burning hot peppers. After several attempts with the chopsticks, I got pretty good, although I had to revert to using my spoon in order to get enough food. After dinner, we sat back and smoked. I went back to my CP and returned with four cans of Coke. We enjoyed the break from the daily routine.

In halting English, Huong talked of his home in Hanoi. At the age of twelve, he had carried supplies for the Viet Minh, who fought against the French, successfully defeating them at Dien Bien Phu. As a truck driver, he had come down the Ho Chi Minh Trail two years earlier. Traveling eight weeks from way station to way station in Laos and Cambodia, he finally arrived at a camp near the South Vietnamese border in Kontum Province. There he had joined a local VC unit and fought in several battles against the South Vietnamese Army that protected Special Forces camps near the borders. Wounded during an airstrike, Trung Sĩ Huong had been captured by the South Vietnamese Army, interrogated, and sent to a prison near Pleiku. After a few months of "re-education," he had decided to join the Chieu Hoi program. He figured his chances of survival would be much higher and he might get a chance to see his family again once the war was over. He translated for the other two scouts. They talked of their hardships in the jungle and how they missed their families. They had been conscripted by VC cadre and given the choice of fighting or being killed along with their families. They too had been captured and later became Hoi Chans. Neither knew where their brothers and sisters were. Both sets of parents had been killed in their villages during fighting between South Vietnamese soldiers and the VC.

I excused myself and went to check my bunker line security for the evening. A half hour later, as I lay down for a few hours of sleep, I could hear the scouts still quietly talking several feet away.

◆　　　◆　　　◆

"Lieutenant, Lieutenant, wake up! We've got movement in front of first squad's listening post."

I opened my eyes to look up into the face of my RTO. Immediately alert, I sat up and reached for my boots. I shook them out and, as I pulled them on, I asked, "Any idea how far away or how many?"

"Negative, sir. Just got the alert from First Squad leader. He's on the radio with the LP now."

I quickly glanced at my watch in the dim moonlight. It was 2:35 in the morning. "OK. Lead the way." We quietly moved towards the first squad's section of the perimeter. I kneeled down behind the squad leader's bunker. "Sergeant Lane, what's the situation?"

"The LP reported movement to his front at thirty or forty meters. Sounds like two or three individuals."

"Who's out there?"

"Watkins and Shorter. Call sign Lima One Alpha."

I radioed the information to the company commander and reached for the squad radio. "Lima One Alpha, this is Three-Six. If you hear me, beep once."

The small receiver in my hand beeped once. Yes.

"Good. If you still have movement beep two times."

Two beeps on the squad radio this time.

"OK. How far in front of your location? Beep once for ten meters, twice for twenty meters, and so on."

The radio responded three times. "Is that thirty meters? Once for 'yes' and two for 'no.'"

One beep.

"Can you talk?"

Two beeps. No. OK. Movement thirty meters from the LP position. Too close for Watkins to talk into the radio without being detected.

"Sergeant Lane, make sure your squad members all know exactly where the LP is located and not to fire in that direction in case we have to bring them in."

"Roger, sir. I'll double check now." He hurried off to make sure everyone was aware that the LPs might be coming in and not to shoot.

Suddenly a relieved voice on the radio whispered. "Monkeys. They're monkeys!"

I spoke into the radio. "Are you sure that it's only monkeys? Anything else out there?"

"Pretty sure, Three-Six. I saw them in the trees just now."

"OK, but remain quiet. Let's make sure those monkeys weren't stirred up by VC crawling through the brush. Just hang tight and no voice traffic for now. Out."

The radio beeped once. Yes.

We waited in the dark for a while listening for more movement. Occasionally we heard movement off in the distance, and once we thought we heard something fall down with a muffled thump. The stars overhead provided a little light. I looked through the starlight scope but saw nothing out of the ordinary. The LPs remained quiet.

"Sir, the CO is on the radio for you," said my RTO as he handed me the handset. Next to him was Platoon Sergeant Singleton.

"This is Three-Six. Over."

"This is Six-One. One hundred percent stand to at 0500. All elements bring in your Lima Papa's at 0515 hours. How copy? Over." The CO had ordered each platoon to withdraw their LPs and have all personnel up and awake, armed, and on the bunkers. Something was up.

Six-One spoke again. "All Sixes report to my location ASAP." That meant all platoon leaders were to join him immediately.

As we assembled in the darkness at the company CP, CPT Trotter began to speak. "All right, listen up. We have movement on two sides of our defensive perimeter. First Platoon LPs reported monkeys moving around. Third Platoon had movement, but he doesn't think it's monkeys and his LPs heard dinks talking." He paused then began to lay out his plan. "If there's more than monkeys out there, we're going to catch them off guard. Exactly thirty minutes prior to BMNT, I will signal to fire a mad minute."

"Sir, what's a mad minute?" asked Lieutenant Mercer, the new platoon leader of Second Platoon.

"It's a technique used to catch Charlie off guard with massive, timed automatic fires. Each rifleman will fire two magazines directly in front of his bunker. Have them fire into the tree line seventy-five to one hundred meters out. Each M79 grenadier will fire three rounds at the same distance. Machine gunners will hold their fire. I don't want to give away their positions. The signal to begin firing will be a red star cluster, the same as final protective fires. The signal to halt will be a white parachute flare. Any questions?"

Mercer asked, "Do we fire claymore mines?"

"No. Do not fire claymores. Any other questions?"

No one had questions, so Trotter said, "To recap, stand to is 0500 hours. At exactly 0515, bring all LPs back into the perimeter. Once their return is confirmed, I'll fire the red flare. Watch closely and keep control of your men. I don't want anyone hurt from our own fires. Got it?"

We all agreed.

"OK. Get back to your platoons and prepare. I want everyone fully awake before we execute this."

I looked at my watch. It was 0450. Sergeant Singleton and I began to go around awakening our soldiers. A short while later, we had everyone up and alert as we radioed our LPs to return into the perimeter. Slowly and quietly, the LPs returned through the concertina and tanglefoot barbed wire. I watched as the shadowy crouched figures safely returned. Everyone watched carefully to see if any other figures followed our men, as Charlie sometimes used this tactic to get in close before detection.

At precisely five thirty, the whoosh of the red star cluster sounded as it rose overhead. A loud pop and bright sprays of fiery red streamers and white smoke followed it. The sky briefly lit as the flare glowed above the treetops. Before the flare extinguished, the night erupted with automatic weapons fire, loud "plops" of 40mm grenades exiting their tubes, and distant explosions as they impacted in the wood lines around the perimeter. Flashes of light made the scene look surreal, as though flashbulbs from hundreds of cameras were snapped one after the other. Red tracers streaked through the night. Silhouettes of soldiers, trees, and bunkers blinked all around us. Soldiers shouted as they fired, adding to the prearranged mayhem.

I could feel the sounds pounding my body as they nearly deafened me. Slowly the firing lessened as soldiers expended their allocated rounds of ammunition. As the firing began to die away, a single white flare popped overhead, signaling the end to this maddening turmoil. All I could think of while standing there in the darkness again was that it was so quiet now that I must have lost my sight as well as my hearing.

"Jesus," said one soldier standing twenty feet to my right.

"Awesome," said another.

"Ouch," said another as he touched the front of his rifle. "This damned barrel is hot."

"OK. At first light, everyone pick up your brass. We don't want Charlie reloading it and using it against us, do we?" Sergeant Singleton's words brought us back to reality. I don't know whether Charlie actually did reload brass shells, but I did know that he could make some dangerous shrapnel out of it in a booby trap if he wanted.

Light was just beginning to show in the distant sky. I was hungry and wanted a hot cup of coffee. "Well, Sergeant Singleton, I guess we now have to make sure these men clean and oil their weapons once they cool off. I'm going to the CP. Back in a minute."

As soon as it was light enough, we sent out local security patrols to see if we caught Charlie by surprise. We found no bodies, but a few blood trails told us we had wounded something. Monkeys? VC? I never did find out. All blood looks the same. We left the area later that day.

◆　　◆　　◆

At the CP, I was kneeling and tying down the straps on my rucksack so they wouldn't get tangled in the bushes or get caught on the chopper as I exited. I had also secured my grenades, gas mask, and ammo so I wouldn't lose them enroute.

"Lieutenant, we'll go in the same chopper on this mission. I've got the squads broken down into lifts of six each. That's the ACL, or allowable cargo load, for these Hueys." Sergeant Singleton took a drink from his canteen and sputtered, "Those damned iodine tablets sure give this water a stinkin' medicine taste."

I stood up. "Yeah, I try to hide the taste by adding Kool-Aid, but then it tastes like Kool-Aid-flavored medicine. Can't win."

I checked my map and made sure my M16 was on safe. I was ready to go. The squad leaders had been briefed on the mission and their soldiers were ready. All were eager to move out but were a bit apprehensive since this was their first major combat mission since the recent disaster with the Vietnamese Skyraiders.

"OK, Sergeant Singleton. I'm all set." We were in the second lift behind First Platoon. I moved out to the chopper pad with my radiotelephone operator by my side and the platoon medic right behind him. I saw the three scouts on the other side of the pickup zone. They would ride in the next chopper behind us.

The five Huey helicopters returned from dropping off the First Platoon on the landing zone. We closed our eyes and lowered our heads as the whirring blades raised clouds of dust. When they touched down, we ran towards them. Quickly climbing on board, I sat on the floor with my legs dangling off the edge. I sat behind the pilot with the door gunner to my right. Next to me was my medic. The doors had been removed for easy access and quick exit. Singleton sat inside and gave me the thumbs-up that all was set. The copilot looked over his shoulder and the crew chief manning the M60 machinegun signaled that we were ready to take off. Loading had taken less than thirty seconds.

We lifted off and headed toward the LZ several clicks away. We were flying two hundred feet above the treetops and moving fast. I enjoyed the ride and the cool air rushing through the chopper.

The countryside was beautiful. The jungle foliage was lush, and the flat terrain was crossed with dirt roads and trails. Below us I saw rice paddies and streams and, in the distance, an occasional small village with thatched huts. The other choppers trailed us, giving me a sense of security. Fifteen minutes into the flight, I saw green smoke on the ground ahead marking the landing zone. First Platoon was already on site. That meant the area was secure and we didn't have to worry about going into a "hot" LZ. No enemy sighted.

The chopper began banking to the right, preparing for the landing a quarter of a mile ahead. Caught off guard, I slowly felt myself sliding toward the open door. I shifted my M16 into my right hand, and with my left I reached for something to hold onto. My rucksack was in the way and I couldn't get my arm up to grab the doorframe as I continued to slide forward. The door gunner was looking in the opposite direction as the chopper began a steeper roll to the right, aligning its approach to the LZ.

I leaned back, attempting to slow my forward movement. In another three seconds I would be out the door, and we were still two hundred feet above the treetops. I opened my mouth to yell.

"Hold on, Lieutenant," I heard Sergeant Singleton shout. He saw my dilemma and grabbed the frame of my rucksack. "Where do you think you're going?" He pulled me backwards into the chopper as my medic grabbed my right arm and helped pull me back inside. I reached up and grabbed the doorframe. My platoon sergeant and medic had prevented my fall to a certain death. As I muttered "Thanks," the chopper leveled out and I got a more secure hold. My first mission almost ended too quickly for me. There was no time to be scared. We had arrived at the LZ.

The chopper hovered a few feet above the ground. I looked down at the elephant grass, judged the distance to the ground, and jumped. The ground was farther than I had estimated and I was surprised when my legs collapsed under me on impact. Unhurt, I took a deep breath, stood up, and headed for the trees at the edge of the LZ. My body and dignity were both bruised, but I had survived my first combat air assault mostly intact.

Sergeant Singleton caught up with me and joked, "Lieutenant, I know you're anxious to get this mission started, but you didn't need to get off the chopper three hundred meters before it landed."

"Believe me, Sergeant Singleton, I sure didn't plan the early exit. Thanks, again. You saved my rear."

"No problem. Didn't need another platoon leader this soon. You just got here."

"Well, I sure appreciate it. Now, let's get these men in position."

"Right."

For the next several hours we prepared hasty positions and waited for the night movement to the hamlet a few kilometers distant. It was a good night for it. There would be no moon to betray our movement.

At midnight I gave the order. "OK. Move out quietly. Keep in sight of the soldier in front of you."

As I walked in the darkness, I listened to the night's stillness, hoping my steps in the brush couldn't be heard. We were beginning to move into our final positions for the cordon around the hamlet. My platoon was in a single file, or "ranger file," as we called it, because there was so little light that it was difficult to see. I couldn't see the soldier in front of me. I reached out with my left hand to touch the soldier ahead of me, as did the soldier to my rear. That way, theoretically, no one would get lost and we could quietly move into position.

Behind me was Mac, my radiotelephone operator, with his radio handset right up to his ear. That way he could keep the volume turned low and still monitor the radio while he listened for instructions from the company commander. I had instructed my squad leaders to maintain radio silence until the search began or we were discovered, whichever came first. So far we had not been discovered. The soldier in front of me was one of my M79 grenadiers and, as he was six feet, four inches, I had to reach up in order to place my hand on his shoulder.

We moved slowly through the darkness and my tension increased along with my excitement that all was going so well on my first combat mission.

Suddenly a tangle of vine halted me in my steps. I started to tell the grenadier in front to of me to hold up and wait for me to get untangled but decided not to make any noise that might give us away. I struggled free and began walking again while reaching out for the shoulder of my grenadier guide. I could hear someone moving slowly in the bushes ahead, although I might as well have had my eyes closed. I could see only blackness ahead.

Increasing my pace and feeling the hand on my shoulder from behind me, I closed the gap between me and the soldier moving just ahead. As my hand touched the soldier in front of me, I breathed a quiet sigh. However, something didn't feel right. The soldier in front of me was much shorter than my grenadier was, and his uniform's texture was different. I whispered. "Who is this?" Back came a reply in Vietnamese.

Oh, shit! Việt Cộng! I thought. Fear immediately replaced the thought, *Where is my KABAR?* I kept my knife taped upside down to my web harness on my left shoulder. I would probably cut my own throat with it in the dark while attempting to remove it from the sheath, but I sure couldn't fire my weapon and give us all away.

I tightened my grip on the uniform of the Vietnamese soldier in front of me and prepared to wrestle him to the ground. But before I had time to execute that move, Huong, the Kit Carson Scout, whispered back over his shoulder to me, "Thiu Úy, not so tight."

Relief overcame me and I exhaled slowly. Releasing the grip on my knife, I replied, "Uh … OK … sure." I felt the sweat running down my face and down the middle of my back. I hoped that the friendly scout hadn't sensed my fear or my plan to silently end his walk through the jungle. As we continued and began to move into position for our encirclement of the hamlet, I rubbed my wedding ring with my thumb. Luck was still with me. This mission was filled with anxious moments, and we hadn't even seen the hamlet yet.

7
CORDON AND SEARCH

September 1968

W E APPROACHED THE small hamlet in the dark, and it was difficult to determine exactly where the buildings were. We settled quietly into temporary positions and waited until the dawn gave us enough light to move into our final cordon. The air was cool and the stillness was unnerving. A few sounds pierced the night as the inhabitants coughed or shuffled around inside the buildings. From one house, a hungry baby cried for a moment until its mother provided it with nourishment.

The horizon slowly began to turn gray with traces of illumination announcing the beginning of dawn. This was BMNT, or the Beginning of Morning Nautical Twilight. Outlines of buildings were now discernable as we again began to move silently. Within a few minutes we were in our final positions.

We now heard more movement in the hamlet as the inhabitants began to stir. The search teams were in their positions and every soldier was alert for any signs of movement. Weapons were pointed in the direction of the hamlet, covering any potential escape route.

A very loud voice on a speakerphone cut through the air, magnifying an unseen speaker's words in Vietnamese. Although I did not know the exact words spoken, I knew that the villagers were being told to come outside and they would not be harmed. Suspected Việt Cộng in the hamlet were informed that they were surrounded and should lay down their weapons and surrender. No one would be harmed if they cooperated.

The distinct loud crack of an AK-47 automatic weapon interrupted the Vietnamese words coming from the loudspeaker. The firing was a hundred meters off to my right. Immediately an M16 answered, followed two seconds later by an M60 machinegun. The red tracers of the machinegun could be seen as they pierced the grayness and ricocheted off into the sky. Soldiers began to shout and angry Vietnamese voices could be heard. The AK-47, spewing green tracers, fired again on full automatic but was silenced by the resumed firing of several M16s and the lone machine gun. A moment later, another M16 fired.

A moment later, the firing stopped. I could hear the voice of someone shouting orders and saw the movement of several helmeted figures running towards the hamlet.

"Hold your fire, men. Sounds like it's over. Keep a watch on your sector in case anyone tries to break through."

"Three-Six, this is Six-One. Over."

My RTO handed me the handset to my radio. "This is Three-Six," I said.

"Roger, Three-Six. That firing was from the Bravo element on your right. Hold your fire and position. They have one bad guy down, and there may be more headed your way."

"WILCO."

I passed the orders to the squad leaders and resumed waiting. The baby began to cry again and this time the mother couldn't immediately silence it. The cry of hunger was replaced by a cry of fear. Loud noises were all around. The firing in the north had stopped. Several Vietnamese voices called out from the direction of the hamlet. They were answered by Vietnamese commands over the loudspeaker.

A few minutes later, several Vietnamese walked slowly out of the buildings and approached the edge of the hamlet. In the group were two old men, an old lady, and a younger woman holding a baby. A small child walked by her side. Except for the woman with the baby, they held their hands high. Vietnamese National Police quickly moved forward to direct the group to a safe location as the search teams moved into the buildings. It was now light enough that I could see the buildings and the other platoons spread out at the edge of the woodline.

"Sergeant Singleton, I'm going to walk over to the Bravo element and see what's happened. I'll return in a few minutes."

"Roger, sir. Be careful."

I walked toward a group of four soldiers looking down at a figure on the ground. They held their weapons casually and appeared to study the fallen figure. As I walked up to them, a Staff Sergeant said, "Well, sir. There's one who didn't get away."

At his feet lay a Vietnamese man dressed in black pajamas with a US Army pistol belt draped diagonally across his chest. He was wearing sandals, and a straw conical hat lay at his side.

Typical VC clothing. The figure was lying in a grotesque position. He was literally sitting on his own shoulders, having been
cut in two at the waist by small arms fire. It must have been the
M16s and the machinegun I heard firing. As he tumbled from
the impact of the bullets, the lower portion of his body had cat-
apulted over his head and landed on his shoulders. Blood and
intestines were strewn around him.

The sight was horrible, but I couldn't turn away. This was
the first dead body I had seen other than a distant cousin I had
seen in a casket several years before. My cousin had been killed
in a car accident and was prepared for burial by a local funeral
home. Billy had looked like a wax figure and seemed to be at
peace. The Vietnamese at my feet had also died violently and
unexpectedly, but he remained untouched as he had fallen in
battle. The skin was pale, the body frail looking. He was obviously a VC, since an AK-47 lay a few feet away and his Chicom
grenades were still attached to his belt. I felt no anger towards
him, but I did feel a strange sadness.

"What happened?" I asked

"He came running out of that house over there once the
loudspeaker started. The National Police have another VC who
was with him. He's only wounded. They're interrogating him."

A young specialist holding a machine gun said, "Yeah, this
guy came out shooting and we all opened up on him. The guy
behind him kept running, and Staff Sergeant Williams was
behind that tree over there. As the second VC ran by, the Sarge
just stepped out and shot him in the shoulder. He was the lucky
one."

Williams broke in, "I'm not sure that he's that lucky if the
National Police are interrogating him." I had to agree. Williams
continued, "I was aiming at his chest but he moved aside as I

pulled the trigger. He took a round above the elbow, spun around, and fell down. That's when I grabbed his SKS carbine and stuck my rifle in his face. Figured a prisoner might be useful."

"Good thinking, Sergeant. The interrogators are probably thanking you right now."

I looked down at the dead VC again and turned back towards my platoon, thankful that the dead soldier wasn't one of ours. Even so, it was awhile before the sick feeling in my stomach went away.

My RTO walked up to me and said, "LT, the CO called and said our scouts discovered four more VC with carbines hiding in the weeds near the trail about one hundred meters over there."

"Where are they now?"

"The National Police have them. It appears four or five more were wounded and got away. Blood trails are all over the place. They escaped through a tunnel in the cemetery. He said to be alert since there may be more VC in the area."

"OK. Pass the info to the squads."

A search of the hamlet revealed another VC hiding in the ceiling of one building. Several more weapons were captured, including a B40 rocket launcher under a pig trough. The mission was a success, with no friendly casualties.

◆   ◆   ◆

We moved out early in the morning with my platoon in the lead. On point were PFC Wright and Specialist Cruz, M79 grenadier. Cruz had a canister round loaded instead of a 40mm high-explosive round. The effect of the canister round was similar to that of a shotgun: it fired lead pellets and was good at short distances. Wright and Cruz were the best point men there were, and I tended to use them on point too frequently, although they always volunteered.

"Hey, sir, I'd rather be up front busting bush than looking at some guy's back for hours," Cruz explained. "Besides, if we get ambushed, the VC usually let the point men go past before they open up." I couldn't argue with that fact, but often the point men were the first to take fire if they stumbled upon the enemy.

Behind me was my ever-present RTO monitoring the company radio frequency. The handset was clipped to his web gear suspenders so he could keep both hands free. I walked with the lead squad, and Platoon Sergeant Singleton walked at the end of the platoon with the last squad.

"Hey, sir. Sergeant Singleton's on the radio for you." Mac handed me the handset.

"Three-Seven, this is Three-Six. Over." Singleton's call sign was Three-Seven.

"This is Three-Seven. We got a problem. Call a halt and I'll come up front."

"Roger." I signaled for a halt and motioned for everyone to spread out and get down. On the signal, each soldier held up his hand in the prearranged manner. Immediately, each soldier moved off to the side of the trail, kneeled, and faced into the jungle watching for any signs of movement. After a moment, Sergeant Singleton came hurriedly striding up the trail carrying his helmet in his hand. His face was red and his teeth were tightly clenched together except when he muttered "God damn it. God *damn* it."

"What's up, Sergeant Singleton?"

Dropping to one knee, he said, "That damned Third Squad. Sergeant Baker had that FNG James carry the starlight scope and he left it back in the patrol base."

"Just what we need. You just found out? We've been on the move for thirty minutes."

Lighting a cigarette, inhaling deeply, and then blowing the smoke out before he spoke, Singleton said, "Yeah. Baker thought James had it and James thought the other squad had it, so no one bothered to make sure. Baker finally screwed up the courage to tell me. I ought to send him back by himself."

"Yeah, well, we can't do that, so have Baker take a fire team with him to recover it and make sure he takes a radio with him, too. Tell him to be careful. You know Charlie likes to move into our patrol bases behind us to see what they can scavenge."

"It would serve him right if Charlie fired him up. Dumb bastard."

"Tell him to keep in touch over the radio and we'll move slowly until he returns."

Mac said, "Sir, the CO's on the radio and wants to know what's the holdup."

Singleton said, "Hey, sir, I'm heading back that way so I'll tell the CO what's going on. He ain't going to be happy."

"Yeah, I know. Can't let Charlie get that scope though. Trotter'll probably chew my ass when we stop for the night. If we don't recover that scope, I may as well pack my gear and forget any career plans."

"Don't worry, sir. We can open a car lot or restaurant or something together since I'll probably get canned, too."

We both had a laugh as Singleton put his helmet back on and moved down the trail.

I waited for ten minutes and signaled for the point to begin moving again. It was easy moving down the trail. I felt secure since the scouts were ahead of me. They had proven trustworthy and I could rely on them to detect any VC or booby traps.

The scouts pointed out a few *punji* stakes alongside the trail. They appeared to have been placed hastily and weren't well camouflaged. We walked more carefully, since we knew that VC had to be in the area now.

We walked for another hour and Mac called ahead to me, "LT, Sergeant Singleton says that Baker's patrol has returned. They have the starlight scope. No problem. No sign of any VC either."

"OK. Good."

The path opened up into a clear area as we walked out of the overhead canopy. To the left of the trail was a pile of grass about three feet high. It looked suspiciously out of place, and I wondered if something was hidden there. Without stopping, I poked it carefully with my M16 and kicked it with my foot to see if it covered anything. Nothing was hidden inside, so I continued on. I had taken about four steps when I heard one of the men behind me yell, "Snake!"

I turned just in time to see a three-foot bright green bamboo viper slithering into the grass on the opposite side of the trail. The bamboo viper is one of the deadliest snakes in the jungle. Luckily, no one got bitten. We had recently evacuated a soldier who was clearing some bushes with a machete when a small bamboo viper struck at him. Fortunately the snake's fangs had only scratched the back of the soldier's hand as he swung the machete through the tall grass, and he only got enough poison to make him violently ill. He was extremely lucky. The rumor was that the poison was so powerful and quick that only two steps after getting bitten, you were dead.

"Hey, LT, that snake came out of that pile of grass you kicked. You must have woke it up from its nap."

Sounding calmer than I felt, I said, "OK. Guess today's my lucky day. Let's keep moving, and be careful." I shuddered, even though it was a hot and muggy day. Quickly putting the incident out of my mind, I promised myself to take my own advice: *Be more careful, dumbass.*

8
THE VOLCANO

October 1968

THREE CLICKS FROM the Cambodian border, we sat on the rim of an extinct volcano. Thousands of years ago, white-hot lava spewed from the center of the cauldron and flowed down its 900-meter-high slopes. One week ago, NVA antiaircraft gunners used the rim as a base to shoot at the Cobra gunships supporting the beleaguered Duc Lap Special Forces camp. During that attack, the NVA antiaircraft guns had managed to shoot down a US Air Force F-100. Using jeeps, the Green Berets tore out of the camp, fought their way to the pilot, and raced him back to safety.

Earlier in the week, the CO had reassigned me to the First Platoon as their Platoon Leader. It seemed the First Platoon had some disciplinary problems. At first I wasn't sure whether I was assigned there for punishment or as a reward. I was now the senior Platoon Leader in the company. Also, I was due for promotion to First Lieutenant in another week.

We had moved two and a half clicks from our location adjacent to the airstrip and taken up defensive positions to provide security for the SF camp. The air was cool at this height and was a welcomed change from the hot, clammy air that made us sweat profusely. Black volcanic rocks scattered around made walking a real adventure. I had heard more than one soldier curse as he stumbled into a small boulder in the dark.

"Sir, Six-One wants you to report to the CP right away," said Turk, my radio operator.

"OK. The resupply chopper just landed, so I hope there'll be some mail for us."

Grabbing my weapon, I headed for the CP. Arriving there, I saw the CO talking with an individual I didn't recognize. I walked over to Captain Trotter, who said, "Lieutenant Evans. This is your new platoon sergeant, Sergeant First Class Mayer."

"Uh … new platoon sergeant, sir?"

"Yep. Sergeant Singleton is now the acting first sergeant. You know Singleton leaves for home in a couple of weeks? Right? My first sergeant's packed and ready to leave on the next chopper. He's on his way back to the world, too."

"Yes. I guess I did. Just hadn't given it much thought lately. Welcome, Sergeant Mayer."

Extending his hand, Mayer said, "Glad to meet you, sir."

Trotter said, "Mayer just got in country last week and came in on the resupply chopper just a few minutes ago. Take him with you and send Singleton to me. Bring Sergeant Mayer up to speed on the mission and layout here. I'll talk with him in a little while."

"Roger, sir. This way, Sergeant Mayer."

Arriving back at the platoon CP, I spoke to Sergeant Singleton. "Well, Sergeant Singleton. Here's your turtle. Sergeant Mayer, meet Sergeant Singleton." They exchanged handshakes and Sergeant Singleton said, "I'm glad to see you. I've got a few days to help get you settled in before I leave, Mayer."

I spoke up. "Well, not exactly, Sergeant Singleton. The CO says that you are now the acting company first shirt. The first sergeant is departing on the resupply bird this evening. The CO wants you at the CP now."

"In that case, I'll see you both later." Singleton headed off to the company CP.

"Lieutenant, what's a *turtle*?" asked Mayer.

"Oh, that's our word for replacements. It takes forever for them to get here, so they're as slow as a turtle. Get it?"

"Yeah, Sarge. Another term for a new guy in country is FNG," explained Turk. "That's 'Fucking New Guy'. No disrespect intended, Sarge."

"Yeah. None taken. I heard that term at Cam Rahn when I got off the airplane. The guys departing for home let us know that right away. They were all smiles as they walked towards the plane. I'd feel the same way. Just don't let me hear you call me that."

"Sure 'nuff, Sarge," said Turk, quickly turning back towards his radio.

"Several of those guys yelled, 'Short.' What's that mean?"

Turk turned around, anxious to help. "That's what Sergeant Singleton is. Short. Means he's short on time left in country. He's actually a two-digit midget, since he's got less than a hundred days to go. He may even be a one-digit midget."

"OK. Got it."

"Where did you come from, Sergeant Mayer?"

"Just left an Air Defense unit at Fort Hood."

As we talked, I learned that Sergeant Mayer had spent his past twelve years in missile units, mostly in Germany. This was his first infantry assignment since basic training. He was eager to learn, and now it was my turn to pass on my combat skills. Although he was only thirty-seven years old, he was old enough to be the father of most of the soldiers here, me included.

"One-Seven, this is Six-Seven." The radio call sounded over the small external speaker next to the radio. We called it the 'squawk box.'"

"That's for you, Sergeant Mayer. It's Acting First Sergeant Singleton," I said, pointing to the radio.

Mayer picked up the squawk box, flipped the handset upside down, and spoke into the earpiece. "This is One-Seven," he said.

I took the speaker from his hand and set it on the ground. Then I took the handset, reversed it, and handed it back to Sergeant Mayer. I showed him the push-to-talk switch. Sheepishly he squeezed the switch and spoke into the mouthpiece. "This is One-Seven. Over."

"Roger, One-Seven. Report to my location. Over."

"OK ... I mean WILCO. Out."

Sergeant Mayer stood and started to walk over to the CP. "Sergeant Mayer, don't forget your weapon," I said.

"Uh ... Roger, sir. I'll be back in a bit." He picked up Mac's M16 and headed to the CP.

As Mayer sauntered off, I thought, *This is going to be interesting.* I hoped the look on my face didn't betray my thoughts. Although I had only been in country a few months myself, I was considered an experienced combat vet, no longer a green "shave-tail" lieutenant. Turk raised his eyebrows and grinned. "Hey, sir, I didn't say it."

"Maybe not, but we were both thinking it." *FNG*. We all started out that way. Sergeant Mayer would do fine. I hoped.

The company XO, Hank Jenkins, walked up. "Man what a life. No cares. Just lying around drawing combat pay. How do I get such a cushy job?"

Hank's voice brought me back from my daydreaming. Reclining against a small volcanic boulder, I stretched and yawned expansively. "Some of us are just lucky. There are times, though when it's not quite so peaceful."

"Yeah. I know. I heard about the viper, Frank. Got some snakebite medicine for you."

"Hank, it's good to see you," I said as I shook his hand. "Pull up a rock. Did you come in on the resupply chopper?"

He dropped his gear and sat down. Jenkins began digging around in his rucksack. He handed me a carton of Marlboro cigarettes and said, "Yeah. Arrived a few minutes ago." Jenkins had only been in country a few weeks and was assigned as company executive officer since none of the platoon leaders wanted to leave the field. He was anxious to get a rifle platoon. His base camp-clean uniform stood out in contrast to our dirty clothes.

I sat up and said, "How've you been? Enjoying the good life at base camp?"

"It's not bad. Too much BS, though. Inventories, administrative boards, junk like that. Not enough excitement for me. You guys get all the fun. Here's that medicinal painkiller for you," he said as he handed me a quart of Jim Beam whiskey. "Use it sparingly. I'll resupply you next payday. Anything else you need from base camp?"

"Nope. Appreciate the bottle. This ought to last me the rest of my tour." I laughed.

"Hey, LT. You need to listen to this," Turk yelled over to me. "I'm listening to the battalion net. There's a long-range reconnaissance patrol that's reporting three elephants on a trail near them."

"Put it on the squawk box."

The LRRP reported over the radio net that three elephants had been spotted a hundred meters from them near the Cambodian border. The LRRPs said the elephants were slowly moving south over the trail on a ridgeline west of their location, just inside the South Vietnam border. Silhouetted against the sky, the elephants were loaded down with supplies strapped to their backs. No enemy soldiers were spotted. We knew the Montagnards used elephants and had heard that the NVA occasionally used them to bring supplies down the Ho Chi Minh Trail from North Vietnam. Obviously, these elephants were familiar with the route. The battalion intelligence officer reasoned that the enemy had loaded them with supplies, slapped them on their rumps, and sent them unescorted down the trail.

Battalion headquarters ordered the patrol to stop the elephants and take them under fire since it was essential to keep the supplies from reaching the NVA base camp. The patrol reported the elephants' location to the closest artillery battalion, who had orders to fire on them. In the meantime, the patrol was directed to engage them with their small arms. As we listened, the patrol fired on the elephants and reported that their grenadier had hit the trailing one in the rump with an M79 grenade round. The 40mm round had blown its tail off, enraging the elephant but doing no other apparent damage. Artillery rounds started impacting close to the elephants, which began running out of sight. It was unknown whether the elephants arrived at their destination. Their route took them back into Cambodia, and the patrol couldn't follow. Sightings of a tailless elephant were reported occasionally near the border over the next several months.

Sergeant Mayer returned from the company CP after an hour and sat down next to the fire. "Hey, Sarge, we've been listening to some LRRPs trying to stop some elephants," said Turk.

"Yeah. I heard it on the battalion radio net. You must be Lieutenant Jenkins, the XO." Mayer stuck out his hand and said, "The CO said to send you back to the CP. The last chopper's heading back to base camp in about ten minutes."

"OK. Thanks. Well, Frank. See you later. I had better talk to the CO and see if he has any last-minute instructions for me. By the way, have you given any thought to switching jobs with me?"

"The CO spoke to me about it, but I'm not ready yet to leave the platoon. Just beginning to feel like I have a handle on things. Thanks anyway. See you soon."

"All right. So long. See you next trip."

As Sergeant Mayer poured a cup of coffee into his canteen cup he said, "Sergeant Singleton has been bending my ear about the platoon and giving me some pointers, LT. I guess I have a lot to learn."

"Hey, don't worry about it. I was as green as they come a few months ago. You'll catch on quickly. Just ask if you have any questions. Turk, my smartass radio operator, is actually a good guy, and he'll help you, too. Right, Turk?"

"Oh, yes, sir. I'll be glad to share my vast combat experiences and knowledge, Sergeant Mayer. By the way, can I have my weapon back?"

Mayer looked at the weapon and sheepishly handed it over as Turk handed Mayer's weapon to him. "Guess I was in a hurry," said Mayer.

"Next to me, Turk is probably the most informed member of the platoon, since he receives and answers most of the radio transmissions from the company. That's why he stays close to me."

"Good. In that case, I'll get rid of the FNG handle pretty quick, right Turk?" Mayer grinned at Turk.

"Hey, you didn't hear it from me," Turk said grinning back.

"Let's walk the perimeter and meet the squad leaders," I said as I stood up.

I introduced Mayer to the three squad leaders and showed him our defensive perimeter and security devices. He was particularly interested in the Echo-8 gas dispenser. It was filled with gas canisters and could be fired with a lanyard pull cord or electronically using a claymore charging handle. It shot out the small canisters over a fifty-meter area and released CS gas.

"I wondered why we carried protective gas masks here. Didn't think the VC or NVA used gas. Now I see that we need it to protect us from our own gas," Mayer said.

"That's partially true, but the NVA have employed tear gas on several occasions, although I haven't encountered it yet."

"Guess I'll keep my mask close by."

Slapping mine, which was strapped to my leg, I said, "I use mine for a pillow. That way I know exactly where it is all the time," I said.

We continued to walk the line and I took Mayer over to introduce him to the other platoon leaders and sergeants. Also, I introduced him to the 81mm mortar platoon sergeant.

"These guys are our pocket artillery. They're accurate and fast. We couldn't get along without them. Besides they usually have a cold Coke or two hidden away."

It was dark by then and we all began to settle in for the night. It began raining and it got cold. Real cold. Wrapped in my poncho liner, I was the coldest I had ever been in Vietnam that night even though the temperature probably wasn't less than 55 degrees. The only soldier who wasn't cold was Sergeant Mayer. He hadn't been in country long enough to get acclimated and was more accustomed to cool weather. On the other hand, the heat during the day was going to give him a hard time until he became accustomed to it.

9
LANDING ZONE BASS

October 1968

O UR NEW PATROL base was adjacent to the isolated Special Forces camp at Polei Kleng. My platoon was responsible for securing a portion of the defensive perimeter at LZ Bass surrounding the 175mm howitzer battery south of the camp and the 3500-foot airstrip. My platoon's bunkers faced to the west. The 3500-foot steel plank airstrip was capable of accommodating C-130 aircraft, which routinely supplied the artillery unit, the Green Berets, and us. Polei Kleng Special Forces camp was built in March 1966 as an outpost to stop infiltration by the NVA.

Situated on a level plain, Polei Kleng was surrounded by low-rising hills a few clicks away. Further to the west, I could see the mountains on the border of Viet Nam and Cambodia. The camp was elevated on a small rise on one side of the airstrip.

The lack of vegetation in the camp and around the airstrip made the barren plain appear desert like. A few hundred yards east of us was a strip of vegetation that ran along the streambed. The locale gave the impression of an oasis in the desert. As they went back to their villages nearby, Montagnards routinely traipsed through the area carrying woven baskets filled with clothes washed in the stream or filled with foodstuff they had scrounged from the GIs and Green Berets. Friendly children smiled as they devoured the chocolate candy the troops handed out. They also clutched the offered cans of C-rations as their wary parents watched their children and occasionally reached for a can of food.

One of the benefits of Polei Kleng was the invigorating waterhole, where everything from dirty soldiers to armored personnel carriers and deuce-and-a-half trucks were washed. Vietnamese Special Forces soldiers, GIs, and Montagnards shared the pool. The local Montagnard villagers made a fair living selling trinkets and colas to the US soldiers routinely on security there. As I later discovered, some of the industrious local young women who washed their clothes in the stream made a few extra piasters servicing the soldiers in the nearby bushes when the sergeants and officers weren't looking. I found this out one day after departing Polei Kleng when I overheard one of my young soldiers bragging to an FNG. The newly assigned soldier exclaimed, "Hey, Sarge, when do you think we might get to go back to Polei Kleng? I hear the boom-boom's pretty good there."

That soldier and his friend got an earful from Sergeant Mayer about VD, VC spies, and immoral behavior. I'm not sure how much of the thunderous on-the-spot counseling was for my benefit, but the secret about Polei Kleng was exposed.

Now I knew why all the young soldiers suddenly had to bathe every day while we were there. I guess that was the cleanest my soldiers were during the whole time they were in Vietnam.

While providing local security for the howitzer battery, our infantry troops conducted local short-range patrols, or SRPs. These patrols were normally one or two clicks away from the patrol base and lasted two or three days.

We were reinforced by a company of M113 armored personnel carriers, or APCs. A benefit of that relationship was the added .50-caliber machine gun firepower these tank-like vehicles brought to us, but, more importantly, they also seemed to carry an unlimited supply of soft drinks and beer. And, even better, ice! Their seemingly endless supply of rations and sodas outweighed the unwanted attention that the APCs usually brought, in the form of incoming mortar rounds (these vehicles were a favorite target of the VC and NVA). We didn't resent the extravagant prices the armored troops charged for these luxuries either. We were glad to get them.

For their own protection, the crews of the M113s erected a tall chain-link screen around the front of their vehicles. This screen gave them a measure of protection from the B40 rockets frequently fired at them. The idea was that the rockets would explode on the chain-link fencing before they hit the carriers. This simple device was highly effective. Each M113 carried several rolls of chain link, metal engineer stakes, and rolled-up concertina tied on the top and sides of their carriers as they moved from site to site.

Returning from the waterhole, I heard someone call my name from seventy-five meters ahead.

"Lieutenant Evans. Lieutenant Evans." PFC Barrett was jogging in my direction.

"Here. What's up?" I called as he neared.

"Sir, Sergeant Mayer sent me to get you. One of our patrols is in contact and he needs you at the CP."

I quickly ran to the CP and saw Sergeant Mayer talking on the radio. "One-Six Alpha, give me your status. Over."

Over the nearby speaker, I heard Sergeant Long, the patrol leader, excitedly reporting to Platoon Sergeant Mayer. "Roger. We just opened up on two Victor Charlies that approached our location. They were chasing a chicken. One was armed with an AK-47 and both were wearing black pajamas. One of them had a sandbag slung over his shoulder. We exchanged fire and they *di di'*d. Over."

"Did you hit anyone?" Mayer asked.

"Yeah. We wounded the one with the sandbag, but he got away. The other one took off in the other direction. We have no casualties, but it shook us up a bit. They just showed up on the trail twenty-five meters in front of us. Over."

Taking the handset, I said, "This is One-Six. What is your location, and do you need redleg? Over." "Redleg" meant artillery support.

"Negative, One-Six. They are long gone and I'm not sure where they went. Break. Current location is six hundred meters west of checkpoint Apache. Break. Request we rejoin your location as our position has been compromised. Over."

"Roger. Head this way and give me hourly SITREPs so we know when you're getting close. Over."

"WILCO. By the way, One-Six, we took a prisoner. Over."

"I thought you said both of them got away."

"Well, the dinks did, but like I said, they were chasing a chicken when they stumbled on our location. The dinks got away, but the chicken didn't. It took a couple of rounds. Don't think it's going to make it. Over."

"At least someone can shoot. Guess that's your reward. See you in a few hours."

10

RHADE VILLAGE

November 1968

CAPTAIN TROTTER ADDRESSED his platoon leaders, "Watch out for punji stakes. Recon saw them along each trail into the village. Probably some booby traps, too. We'll go slow and stay on the trail until we move into our final positions. We'll announce our presence just before first light."

"Are the White Mice working with us again?" asked Lieutenant Jenkins.

Yeah, the National Police will link up with us once we're in our positions. They'll interpret through a local Montagnard tribesman. We have reports that the local VC recruit young men from the area and sneak back into this village to spend the night. These villagers are basically neutral; we don't want to hurt any of them. I want you to control your fires very closely."

Once again, our primary mission was to cordon and search a suspected VC hideout. This time we would encircle a small Rhade village of about twenty huts. The Rhade tribe lived in thatched-roof huts built on stilts about five feet above the ground. These primitive dwellings were similar to others we had seen, such as the Jarai ones near Kontum. Many tribes shared similar customs and worshiped the spirits of fire, water, and wind. They practiced the ritual of using a matchmaker or family member to propose marriageable women to men. In the Rhade culture, the oldest or most respected woman usually ruled the household.

We moved out just before midnight. Keeping close together in the dark, we made little noise, since my squad leaders had secured all loose equipment with tape and then checked it. We had to remain quiet if we expected to sneak into position around the village. All went well and there was just enough moonlight for us to see the trail we followed. We walked three hours, then halted.

Captain Trotter called on the radio and informed the three platoon leaders that we had reached our initial positions. He called us to his CP. "OK, men, I want absolute silence from this point forward. It's essential that we're not discovered. I want you to keep close control of your weapons, and don't fire unless threatened. Got it?" We all nodded. "Let me know when you're in position and linked up with units on either side of you. No radio traffic until then. Again, keep noise to an absolute minimum. We move out in fifteen minutes."

I returned to my platoon and prepared to move. All was quiet. Occasionally I heard small noises coming from the village and wind rustling the leaves. Good. The wind would help cover any movement noises we might make. Finally in position, I radioed to the CO. "Six-One, this is One-Six, in position. Over."

"Roger. Out."

Now all we could do was wait. One of the huts was twenty yards in front of me. Smoke and the smell from pigs and goats milling around under the hootches wafted through the air. The blowing wind chilled us. Lying on our stomachs, we watched for any signs of movement. I breathed as quietly as possible. It was nearing five thirty in the morning, and the villagers would soon be preparing for the day's schedule. More importantly, if there were any VC in the village, they would be preparing to slip back into the jungle before sunrise.

Suddenly I heard a cough and shuffling sounds from inside the hut. I pointed my rifle at the doorway and looked through my sights. In the dim moonlight, I saw a small figure step out. It walked to the edge of the log porch and stared right at me. I held my breath and stared back. It was a ten-year-old girl in an ankle-length skirt of rough hand woven fabric and a short sleeve shirt. Her black hair was cropped short. She reached down, raised her skirt above her knees, and spread her feet apart. I heard splashing through the wooden porch and the grunt of a pig under the floor as it quickly moved out of the way. The girl finished, dropped her skirt, stretched and yawned, and returned to the hut. Although she seemed to be looking right at me, she hadn't seen me. I took a deep breath and exhaled slowly, feeling confident the villagers hadn't detected us.

Waiting was difficult. No one moved in the cool night air. Gradually the sky began to turn gray. In the distance a rooster crowed. Almost simultaneously, I saw two shadows on the platform of the hut on my left. They were crouching and moving very slowly. They dropped to the ground and I heard a voice in

Vietnamese shout, "*Dung lai! Dung lai!*" Stop! Stop! Immediately I heard another voice calling in a language I didn't recognize. That must have been the interpreter calling for the figures to halt. Both figures stopped moving for a split second, then turned around and ran toward the center of the village. One of the retreating men was carrying something. Overhead a parachute flare popped and the night briefly became daylight. Shouting from the village mixed with strident Vietnamese commands, flooding the night. Another flare popped overhead, and I saw a large thatched hut in the center of the village. That was the communal house, where ceremonies and meetings of the village elders were held. Beyond the large hut I could see movement as the search teams rushed forward to locate any VC trapped inside the cordon. Not a shot had been fired.

"All units hold your positions on the perimeter while the search teams check the village," the CO ordered over the radio. "We have taken two suspected VC and there may be more in hiding."

"Sergeant Mayer," I called, "make sure we have security to our rear. I don't want to get caught off guard."

"Already taken care of, sir."

"Roger. Let's sit tight and keep our eyes open."

Forty-five minutes later, the hut-by-hut search was complete. It was now dawn, and I could see all the villagers grouped in the center of the village. The National Police were tying a VC suspect's hands behind his back. They placed him on his knees next to the other two captured earlier. They placed him on his knees next to the two other prisoners. One weapon, a Chinese made SKS, was discovered along with two Chicom grenades, hidden under a grass mat near the well.

With the interpreter's help, a Vietnamese National Police Lieutenant questioned two of the village elders, an old man and an ancient woman. The thin interpreter in the tiger-stripped uniform angrily asked a question, and the old man said something to the woman. She snapped a quick response and gestured toward the VC suspects. Again the old man spoke, and the woman diffidently spoke to the interpreter as she pointed to a pile of wood stacked near the communal house.

Quickly the interpreter spoke to the Vietnamese officer, who shouted to his men. Two policemen ran to the woodpile and pointed their weapons at the stack. One of them spoke loudly in Vietnamese. The other one reached down and pulled a straw mat away from the woodpile, uncovering a man hiding in a spider hole. He raised his hands and was roughly pulled to his feet and dragged over to join the other suspects. His hands were tied like the others. The prisoners looked terrified. They all appeared to be in their mid to late twenties and were dressed in peasant clothing, including sandals made of rubber tires. The villagers were questioned for another hour then the Vietnamese officer in charge gestured toward the prisoners and spoke a command to his men. The four VC suspects were pulled to their feet and bound together with a length of rope. They appeared relieved to be tied up. I suspected that they were grateful they hadn't been shot on the spot. After several minutes a helicopter arrived and landed in the nearby clearing. The White Mice pushed their captured VC suspects aboard the chopper, climbed onboard behind them, and left for in-depth interrogation in Ban Me Thout.

The villagers, with obvious relief, returned to their huts while we prepared to move to our night location. Some of the soldiers passed out candy to the children and others handed their unwanted C-rations to the older villagers.

The CO ordered, "Move out!" and we followed the trail out of the village.

Next morning, Alpha Company was assigned a new first sergeant and my old mentor, Sergeant Singleton, left for home. I remember the day he climbed on the chopper for the ride back to the base camp. He and I had shared many experiences and he, more than any other, had helped me transition from a green, inexperienced lieutenant to a jungle savvy combat leader. I knew that I had passed his approval as he waved from the chopper and shouted, "So long, Frank. Good luck." It was a personal message that went against protocol. Sergeants don't normally call officers by their first name, just as officers don't call sergeants by their first name. It's too familiar and can erode the mutual respect each should show to the other. In this case, it was natural and gave me a feeling of pride and accomplishment. I had passed muster with a respected, trusted comrade. I had measured up.

11
CAMP ENARI

December 1968

THE CO WAS talking on the radio as I approached. "WILCO. Six-One, out." He looked up as I arrived and said, "Grab a seat, Frank." He reached for his hot cocoa and began stirring it with a stick. How could he drink that stuff in the heat of the day? I couldn't understand. Give me a cold Coke anytime. Satisfied with a swig of water from my canteen, I sat on the log near the small fire.

The Second and Third Platoon leaders, along with the artillery forward observer, were seated in a circle awaiting the CO's next words. Rumor was that we would be going in for a short break to Camp Enari. I looked forward to the hot chow, cold beer, and clean jungle fatigues. Everyone looked tired but hopeful.

Looking exhausted, Captain Trotter said, "Gents, we are heading for LZ Bass to secure the 175mm artillery battery there." Trotter could see the disappointment in our eyes. "We'll be sending out short-range patrols to VC Valley. We hope to locate the NVA regiment that's reportedly moving over the Plei Trap Road." He paused and looked at each of us. Smiling, he added, "First, however, we are going to the division base camp for a two-day stand down and refit."

"Yeah! Good deal!" said Lieutenant Mertz, the Third Platoon leader, echoing our thoughts and bringing smiles to all our faces. "Can't wait to get these stinky fatigues off and scrub the crud off my body."

"We can't wait for you to do that, too," spoke Jim, the artillery FO. "I've been trying to stay upwind of you for the past week."

"OK, men, that'll do. We all need a good shower and clean clothes. A thick steak wouldn't hurt either. Wash it all down with a cool Tiger Beer or two."

"Captain, when do we leave?" I asked.

"The CH-47s will be here around 1400. Time to break down and pack up. I want all bunkers collapsed, sandbags emptied, trash buried, and concertina wire picked up. Don't leave a thing that Charlie can use."

We quickly left to pass the good news to our platoons. The men deserved a break, and life would be much easier with a couple of days of rest and hot food. Also, we were told that mail was waiting for us back in base camp. That brought everyone's spirits up even more.

The choppers arrived and we climbed aboard for the ride to Enari. As loud as the chopper noises were, almost everyone fell asleep within a few moments. I leaned back and dozed too as

fatigue took over my body. We landed at the airstrip and transferred to deuce-and-a-half trucks for the short ride to the brigade area. During the convoy, everyone was alert and carefully
observed the woods along the roadside for anything suspicious.
Ambushes were commonplace in this area and mines were frequently placed in the roads. We arrived without incident.

"OK, gentlemen, listen up," I said to my squad leaders. First
order of business is to make sure all weapons are unloaded and
on safe. I want you to personally inspect all weapons chambers
to make sure they are clear and no magazines are in the weapon.
It's the old 'No brass, no ammo, Sergeant.' Remember how we
did it on the ranges during training?"

"Sir, I'll check the squad leaders and headquarters." Sergeant
Mayer raised his voice and spoke so all could hear. "Also, men, I
want all weapons cleaned before you head to the showers.
There's burn barrels over there for your trash." Sergeant Mayer
indicated the smoking fifty-five gallon barrels thirty yards away.
"After weapons inspection, I'll release each squad to go to the
shower point. The first squad to get their weapons cleaned and
trash burned gets to shower first. After showers, head to the
mess hall, where they're cooking steaks for us. Squad leaders
stick around for a few minutes; I have some more instructions
for you."

I left the platoon sergeant to instruct the squad leaders and
walked over to the officer's quarters. The wooden barracks had
bunk beds with clean sheets and pillows. This would be the first
time I had slept in a bed for nearly four months. I dropped my
gear and peeled off my clothes. Wrapping a towel around me, I
headed to the shower. There was even a little hot water. As I
stood under the cascading water, it relaxed my muscles, opened
my skin pores and I almost forgot where I was for a time. The

warmth of the water running down my body and the soft splashing of the spray evoked a sense of calmness that I hadn't felt for many weeks. I forced myself to turn off the water and towel off. Refreshed, back in the barracks I picked up my clean fatigues and dressed. I felt re-energized and ravenous. I was ready for a couple of thick, blackened steaks now. If they weren't fully cooked yet, I might rip one off the grill and eat it raw.

An explosion sounded of to my left as I stepped outside. Thinking it was an incoming mortar round, I dived to the ground. Expecting another explosion, I looked around and saw several people running toward one of the fire barrels. It was blown apart. Fire and ashes littered the ground. A few feet away, a soldier I didn't recognize was near the remains of the barrel. He looked stunned. Fortunately, he didn't appear hurt.

The Second Platoon medic ran over to the soldier and helped him sit on the ground. He began checking him out to determine injuries.

"What happened?" I asked.

Sergeant Mayer said, "I think a 40mm grenade exploded in the fire. Must have gotten thrown in the trash by accident. Damned stupid accident."

"Yeah, fortunately there's no major injuries. Looks like the soldier will be OK. Let's keep everyone away from the barrels for now. Looks like they've pretty much finished burning their trash anyway. Here's the MPs so they can take charge and figure out what's happened." That incident reminded me that anywhere in a combat zone, it was dangerous to let your guard down. Too many soldiers were injured or killed from such accidents.

The remainder of that day and the next were uneventful—we wrote letters, slept, ate, and spent a few hours each evening at the small officers' club. As comfortable as the rear area was compared to the "bush" where I had spent the past several months, I was ready to get back into the jungle. I couldn't explain it; I guess I was becoming bored. Most of the troops were ready to leave also.

The third morning we loaded onto trucks and departed for Kontum, then on to Polei Kleng. We would patrol the area west of the Special Forces camp. If we were lucky, we would locate the NVA regiment and stop their infiltration south.

12
PLEI TRAP VALLEY

November 1968

THE SLICK LANDED on a barren hilltop adjacent to the rutted dirt road that wound through the countryside. I jumped off the Huey onto a hilltop bare of vegetation. Once forested hills, the landscape was now desolate and lifeless. No leaves hung from the dead trees, and the ground was void of grasses. The crumbly, orange clay earth was scorched with patches of deadfall strewn everywhere I looked. Agent Orange had swept all life from the countryside.

The area had been bombed by B-52 "Arc Light" airstrikes. The burned and broken tree trunks stuck up five or six feet into the air. Their splintered limbs were further evidence of the violence that ripped through the landscape. Here and there were clumps of shriveled bushes and the splintered tree limbs were tossed about as if a devil's fiery breath had blown everything askew. Craters ranging from a few feet to thirty feet in diameter pitted the road and pockmarked the hills. I was standing on the infamous Ho Chi Minh Trail. This was the major supply route used for decades by the Viet Minh and later the North Vietnamese Army as it infiltrated troops into South Vietnam.

The trail supported traffic by foot, bicycles, mules, elephants, trucks, and tanks. Alongside the trail was evidence of campfires, bamboo shelters, and shallow bunkers used by the NVA soldiers as they infiltrated south. They used the trail to move provisions and reinforcements day and night to keep the NVA supplied. Frequently pilots reported seeing vehicle headlights and flashlights winding down this jungle highway across the borders in Laos and Cambodia. Air Force planes dropped tons of bombs every month along the trail in South Vietnam to interdict the flow of men and materiel, but the damages were quickly repaired by thousands of laborers within a few hours of each strike.

Our mission was to patrol the Plei Trap road and interdict the enemy convoys using it. With luck, we could prevent, at least for a while, the movement of supplies. The area we landed in had been recently bombarded by friendly artillery and Cobra rockets to clear out the enemy soldiers in the vicinity. We landed without resistance. Even so, the enemy was close by. If we found them, we didn't know whether they would stand their ground for a fight. Usually they only held their ground in a fight when they had a vastly superior advantage in numbers.

Walking south down the trail I saw craters in the dirt road large enough to hold a dump truck. Evidence was everywhere of smaller craters that had been filled in. I imagined hundreds of laborers using shovels, bamboo hats full of dirt, and bare hands to fill in the damaged roadway. In some places, the road just angled around the crater. It had apparently been quicker to build a detour rather than fill in the hole. Tire tracks from vehicles and hundreds of sandals left imprints in the dust.

A story made the rounds that testified to the determination of the NVA soldiers and their willingness to bear unbelievable hardships to support the fighting in South Vietnam. The tale described a skinny, young NVA private who hefted a heavy 120mm mortar round on his back in North Vietnam. Around his neck he carried a cloth tube filled with his ration of rice. A small metal canteen hung at his side. He hadn't been issued a weapon yet; he could pick one up later from one of the numerous casualties he was told he would encounter. Following orders, he began walking down the Ho Chi Minh Trail during the driving rains of the monsoon season. After eight long, arduous weeks of dodging B-52 airstrikes and napalm flames in the knee-deep mud, he finally arrived at his destination in the south. His new unit was battling with a South Vietnamese Army company (Army of the Republic Vietnam or ARVN). He carefully unstrapped the mortar round from his aching back, wiped it dry with the now empty rice bag, and weakly handed it over to a seasoned NVA sergeant standing next to a smoking mortar tube. The sergeant promptly dropped it down the mortar tube, sending it on its way towards the target. Turning to the young ammunition bearer who had just supplied the mortar round, the NVA sergeant said, "Good, Private. Now, go get me another one."

Standing on that infamous trail, I now began to appreciate how difficult the long trek south must have been for the young replacements, supply bearers, and laborers.

We had been patrolling along the trail for only an hour or so when a muffled explosion sounded off to my left. Everyone dropped to the dirt off to the side of the trail. A soldier walking left flank security on the ridge above yelled out. "Mines! There's small mines all over up here."

"Is anyone hurt?" I called back.

"Yeah, but not bad, I think. Johnson stepped on one."

"Call the CO and tell him what happened. I'm going over to the left flank," I told my RTO. Turning to my medic, I said, "Doc, you come with me."

We climbed the small hillside and I saw three soldiers. One was lying on the ground, but he appeared alert. The other two were kneeling and looking at his foot.

"Is Johnson OK?" I asked.

Johnson said, "Hey, sir. I'm OK. My foot stings like hell. I don't think it's broke though. Careful. Those little mines are all over the ground and they're hard to see. There's one over there." He pointed to a small greenish-gray object a few feet away.

It was a flat triangular bag about the size of a hand. It was hard to see. It resembled a beanbag and blended in with the debris and leaves on the ground. At a quick glance, it looked like a shriveled leaf.

Another muffled explosion sounded fifty meters up the trail. Another soldier had stepped on a mine. My RTO had joined us by then. "Turk, tell the squads to be careful where they step and not to sit down without looking at the ground first. Radio the CO, too."

"Roger, sir. Already talked with the CO and he said the same thing. Said be careful where you step. They found some of these mines down the trail a ways, too. They're antipersonnel mines that the Air Force drops along the trail. They activate once they have been rained on and then dried out. They won't cause any major damage to a soldier wearing a combat boot, but they can blow off a foot wearing Ho Chi Minh sandals."

"That's good to know," said Johnson. "My foot is throbbing and feels like it's swelling. Doc, loosen my boot, will you?"

"Let me look first." He examined Johnson's foot and said, "There's no blood. No tear in the boot. I'm going to remove the boot now."

Removing the boot slowly with only a small yelp from Johnson, Doc said, "Can't tell if any bones are broken, but there's no cuts or blood. Sir, I think we still need to medevac Johnson. He can't walk on this for a couple of days even if there's no broken bones. Besides, it will have to be X-rayed."

"OK. Turk, give me the handset." I took the handset and informed the captain that we needed a dustoff chopper. While awaiting the dustoff for the two injured soldiers—Second Platoon had a soldier with a foot injury, too—we carefully located more mines. We counted seventy-four in the short time we were there.

Following the evacuation of the two injured soldiers, headquarters decide to pull us out before we took any more casualties from the mines. As our slick gained altitude, I looked back at the Ho Chi Minh Trail. I was glad that I wasn't one of those NVA soldiers or a conscripted, sandal-wearing laborer walking along the trail in the dark, far from medical help.

13

MAIL CALL

December 1968

A SLICK LANDED on the pad and the door gunner tossed out four bulging bags of mail as the red dust swirled up and plastic sandbags sailed into the air. A soldier with a one hundred two degree fever climbed on board the chopper and it lifted off climbing into the evening sky heading back to Camp Enari.

"Mail call. Come and get'em."

Nothing short of combat raised the level of excitement quite like hearing the choppers inbound with mail. The pilots would usually call ahead and let the company RTO know that he carried mail. There was no hesitation in gathering volunteers to help unload the chopper on the landing pad when it landed. Often, the company first sergeant would have to run soldiers away from the mail-carrying chopper, since it was dangerous for too many individuals to be around the moving overhead blades and whirring tail rotors.

At the platoon level, distribution of mail was the platoon sergeant's job. In those few minutes Sergeant Mayer took to hand out the mail, he had the undivided attention of everyone in the platoon. Occasionally he subdivided the mail into squad piles and allowed the squad leaders to pass it out to their own men, but normally he reserved that right for himself. It was a good opportunity to speak to the assembled group and pass any daily guidance or words of wisdom. Also, he could see first hand who received packages from home and, more importantly, who did not receive mail.

The quickest way to see a soldier's morale to go up was to hand him a letter from home. Likewise, it was depressing for a soldier not to get mail when all those around him were eagerly clutching letters and waiting for more. When that happened, the platoon sergeant, if not one of the soldier's buddies, would make sure that the overlooked soldier got a share of someone's cookies or cake or other goodies from home from what we called our care packages. Everyone shared their goodies with buddies and fellow squad members. It was expected and normally graciously observed.

As the platoon leader, I waited until all the mail had been distributed before I opened my letters. That was the protocol of the times. Often I received my own package of goodies from my wife or my mother. My mother would send homemade peanut butter fudge, which usually lasted no more than a few minutes after it was announced that "the LT has fudge!" Sometimes I was quick enough to hide away a piece or two to eat in solitude with a hot cup of black coffee the next morning. The packaged dried fruit that my wife often sent was a real treat, and one that

I could normally keep to myself as no one else seemed to enjoy it quite like I did. A few days before Christmas in 1968, I was fortunate to get two letters from home and a package from my father-in-law. What a surprise. I had never expected to receive a package from him. Not that he wasn't a wonderful person, but it didn't seem in his nature to send a care package to his new son-in-law. I was excited and wanted to open it quickly.

My father-in-law had served in the army in Panama before World War II and retired as a senior noncommissioned officer in the quartermaster corps. During the war he served in the mountains of Tennessee chasing draft evaders, and later in the Philippine islands. He managed an officers' club in the Philippines for a while and served in supply-related assignments throughout the Korean conflict. Years later, shortly before he retired, he received orders to report to Vietnam. On the way there, he discovered that his accumulated years of service qualified him for an exemption from combat, so he went back to his family in Columbus, Georgia. He had seen the world from Georgia to Panama to the islands of the Pacific to occupied Germany and back. His career spanned thirty-one years, and it was time for others to take up the reins of service.

Eagerly I returned to my bunker with my mail from home. I put the two letters from my wife and my mother in my pocket to read later in private. The package demanded to be open immediately. I saw my platoon sergeant and radio operator watching from a respectful distance, anticipating a share in those goodies from the states. Although I had devoured a C-ration meal only an hour earlier, I was salivating at the thought of cookies, cake, fudge, or some other sweet surprise.

As I cut the box open quickly, I realized then how light this package was. *Oh, well,* I thought, *it's probably candy bars, Rice*

Crispy treats, or some other freeze-dried morsels. Perhaps a book, magazine, or a newspaper from home was inside. I removed the newspaper wrapping and found a large number of folded paper items, bright white in color. As I picked up one of them, I suddenly realized what I held: a white paper cook's hat like those worn by cooks in the army mess halls back in the States, similar to the one I wore as a teenage carhop at a Steak and Shake a few years earlier! I looked down at the box on top of the bunker. As Sergeant Mayer came over to look, I realized that I was the proud owner of 144 white paper cook's hats.

My first reaction was to burst into laughter at my father-in-law's prank.

Sergeant Mayer said, "What the hell?" and laughed along with me. "Well, Lieutenant, just what are we going to do in the jungle all camouflaged up so Charlie won't see us and wearing those damned *white* cook's hats?" I had no answer at that moment.

As I sat there staring at the hats, I realized that this was no joke. No, my father-in-law had sent the gift with an honest intent to demonstrate his support. It said, "We are with you, son." I believe the package from him was a way of saying "Carry on. We're here supporting you until you return." I was comforted then as I realized he probably didn't understand my conditions in Vietnam. If he didn't know, my wife probably didn't know either. That was OK with me, as I never described them in my letters home. He didn't know how much I appreciated the gifts, and especially the thoughts behind them.

Sergeant Mayer walked away muttering, "Hats. Damned *white* hats."

I sat down on the edge of my bunker and smiled. I unfolded the hat I had taken from the box, opened it, and placed it on my head. Sighing, I looked off into the jungle and thought of home.

Would you like fries with that steak burger, sir?

14
LZ CHRISTMAS

December 1968

I T WAS QUIET and the enemy had been elusive the past few days. The National Front for the Liberation (NLF) of Vietnam agreed to a limited cease-fire during the holiday period. One day earlier we had arrived at the aptly named LZ Christmas. This would be our firebase and home for the next week. No one expected the cease-fire to be honored, but we all had hopes. It was Christmas Eve and a resupply chopper with bags of mail and packages was going to land in a few minutes. We had received a resupply of soft drinks and beer, so those not on bunker guard were celebrating. The word was spread that there had better not be any overindulging. We were still in a combat zone and had to stay alert for enemy action. Even so, there was an air of festivity over the firebase.

We had a new company commander. Captain Trotter had finished his tour in the bush and was reassigned to brigade headquarters. Captain Schlusser assumed command during this quiet period.

I was relaxing on my bunker and anticipating the arrival of the mail. One chopper had just landed with the beverages. They were warm but still appreciated. Most soldiers traded their beer for soft drinks. The going exchange rate was two cans of beer for one can of soda, since warm beer was not popular.

As I drank the last of my can of warm Schlitz, the CO's RTO came down the hill holding a large cooked turkey! Since we had been living on C-rations exclusively for several days, the turkey looked even more delicious. I sure hoped that there was dressing to go with the roasted turkey. They could keep the cranberry sauce.

"Sir, here's Christmas dinner," PFC Daley said, grinning widely.

Lying on the bunker next to me was the new KA-BAR that I had received in the mail a few days earlier: a gift from my mother-in-law. I had requested it several weeks earlier, since mine had been lost. I reached for the knife, and as Daley held the bird out to me, I said, "Daley, you get the first piece. Let me cut you a drumstick."

I raised the knife, grabbed the large drumstick, swung the blade, and nearly removed my thumb from the rest of my left hand. I sliced it to the bone at the wrist below the thumb and looked in astonishment as blood spurted all over me and the turkey leg. I dropped the knife and promptly passed out.

The next thing I remember was being carried to a medevac chopper and protesting to be let down. "Hey, sir, you cut the crap out of your hand and it's going to take several stitches to fix it up," said Doc. "Lay still and quit fighting us."

They loaded me on the chopper and all I could think was *Dammit. Not with a new company commander. He'll think I'm an idiot.*

It was a short chopper ride to the division hospital. I walked into the emergency room. The treating physician wished me a Merry Christmas and said, "You're the lieutenant that had a knife fight with a turkey, right?"

"Great. I guess everybody has heard."

A nurse scrubbed the cut area then numbed my hand. I've often wondered why she didn't numb it first? "Combat wound?" she asked. I was too embarrassed to answer and just shrugged. She winked and grinned. "The dustoff pilot told us."

The doctor returned and began to stitch my hand. I had cut the muscle pretty deeply, but he told me that I probably wouldn't lose any flexibility in the thumb.

"Another inch to the left and you would've been carrying that thumb in here in a handkerchief," he said. "You'll need to stay overnight since it's getting late."

"Doc, I need to get back to my unit. I've got a new company commander and I can't be gone long. I look like a dummy already, cutting my hand like this."

He laughed and said, "OK. I understand. You can catch a ride on the deuce-and-a-half outside. It's leaving for the division base camp in a half hour or so. Keep that thumb bandaged and don't use it for about a week." He handed me some pills. "Take these antibiotics and painkillers. It'll hurt like hell for a few days. You'll be back to normal in a couple of weeks. Your medic can remove the stitches later." As I walked out of the door, the doctor called out, "Hey! Watch out for those enemy turkeys from now on." I heard his laughter all the way to the truck. I could imagine the talk at the hospital officers' club that night.

I left on the truck a few minutes later and arrived at the division base camp before dark. I arranged to catch the first resupply chopper to LZ Christmas in the morning. That night, I had a warm shower and walked to the division's officers' club. After a couple of games of liar's dice and a few cold beers, followed by a fish dinner, I began to feel human again. My hand was beginning to throb a little. I felt a guilty for a moment, but it didn't last long.

The next morning I arrived at LZ Christmas. I reported to the company commander and sheepishly explained that I wasn't really that stupid all the time. Captain Shu said, "So I've been told. Heck of a Christmas present, huh?"

I headed back to my platoon CP. Doc saw me and said, "Hey, LT. Want me to put you in for a Purple Heart? That was an enemy turkey, right?"

"Doc, I can't say what I'm thinking right now, so just go away." My hand ached, I had a slight hangover, and I was still embarrassed from my stupid accident. I didn't feel like being kidded at that moment. Doc turned and started to walk away. I called to him, "By the way, thanks for the first aid."

"Sure, LT. I don't get much of a chance to treat knife wounds. I needed the practice. Good, clean slice. Must have been a sharp knife. You should have known to be careful with a knife your mother-in-law sent you." Laughing, he walked back to his hooch.

15
REST AND RECUPERATION

January 1969

A T 3:00 A.M. Honolulu time, the airplane touched down at the International Airport and the noise inside the plane was deafening. We still had a bus ride to the R&R Center at Fort DeRussy, but everyone on the plane was shouting with excitement.

As the plane rolled to a stop, we were instructed to remain in our seats for a quick briefing and instructions on what would happen next. I don't know about the other guys, but I just wanted to rush the door, race down the stairs, and get the show started. No luck. A sergeant from the R&R center came aboard and spoke to us about enjoying our time in Hawaii. He reminded us that we were representatives of the military—we were to conduct ourselves accordingly, stay out of trouble, and report on time for departure for our flight back to Vietnam.

We were all thinking the same thing. *Yeah, yeah, yeah. Let's get moving.*

Once he finished his prepared remarks and stepped out of the way, we were allowed to deplane. We hurriedly loaded onto busses for the short ride through town. No steel mesh covered the windows on these busses. We were "back in the world" now. As we approached the R&R center, my nose was pressed up against the window. I was hoping to locate my wife in the crowd in the distance. All I could see were women everywhere. They were all dressed in their Sunday best, with perfect hair and looking as excited and eager as I felt. Somewhere in that crowd was my very own wife of eight and a half months. I had just spent six of those months in Vietnam and was looking forward to a few days of near normalcy with her on the beautiful island of Oahu. Actually, I was looking for a few days of *frantic and passionate* normalcy on the beautiful island of Oahu.

Sitting about halfway down the aisle, it took me a few minutes to move to the door, where I could look in earnest for my wife. Scanning the crowd of excited, perfectly coiffured females, I couldn't locate her. I walked away from the bus, continuing to look for her familiar face as the soldiers, sailors, and airmen around me began yelling and waving to their wives and girlfriends. I made my way through the crowd, thinking she must have decided to meet me at the hotel or, worse, had missed her flight and wouldn't be there.

Just as I was about to resign myself to a week in Hawaii alone, I heard a penetrating voice behind me: "*Frank … Fraannnk!*" Turning around, I met with an armful of happy, excited, and slightly annoyed wife. "Didn't you see me? I've been chasing you through the crowd," she said.

"No, didn't see you," I said, grinning. I knew better than to tell her that I didn't recognize her at first in that multitude of women. After all, it had been six months since we had last been together. The only picture I had of her was the one in camouflaged pajamas and my beret. We had known each other only three months before we were married. I left for Vietnam three months later. After six months in combat, was it any wonder that I had a little difficulty recognizing her? A passionate kiss left me light-headed and we left arm in arm for the Illikai Hotel.

We checked in and took the elevator to our room. I shut the door behind me and dropped my bags to the floor. Without warning, I was spun around, thrown to the bed, and pinned down by a suddenly very strong female.

"Hey," I protested, "let me take a shower and wash some of this jungle crud off first."

"Later."

We became passionately reacquainted, and sometime later I took my first hot shower in many weeks. As I showered, I was a bit dismayed to see that my attempt to grow a mustache had rapidly disappeared under the soap and hot water. All that was left was thin blond fuzz. A couple of strokes of my razor later and it was gone. My wife didn't seem to mind or notice. She commented upon my loss of the fifteen pounds I had gained shortly after our marriage. Once again, I was a lean 130 pounds.

The next few days went by too quickly. We visited the Don Ho show in the International Marketplace and several other highlights of Oahu. It was unseasonably cool, but neither of us missed swimming at the beach. We enjoyed candlelit dinners, romantic nights, and walks on the beach hand in hand. Both of us fell in love with Hawaii and promised to return one day.

Our last night in Hawaii came too soon. We had a quiet dinner and took a cab back to the hotel. After overhearing that this was our last night in Hawaii and that I was departing back to Vietnam that evening, the cab driver would not accept payment for the ride. I was touched by that act of thoughtfulness. It would be years later before anyone again thanked me for my service in Vietnam. Looking back, I will be forever grateful to that anonymous cabbie for his kindheartedness.

16

THE PUNCHBOWL

January 1969

I LOOKED DOWN between my feet at the ground. *Boy that sure looks like a place I don't want to be,* I thought. Returning from a wonderful week in Honolulu, I was freshly scrubbed, shaven, and although not exactly rested, at least refreshed. Below my inbound chopper I saw hills all around and a clearing of about 150 square meters rimmed with bunkers and a large CP in the center. This was the battalion firebase. I understood why it was named the Punchbowl. Anyone positioned on the rim had a clear view of everything clustered in the depression below: a perfect view of the battalion firebase by an enemy observer or sniper.

I walked from the helicopter landing pad and looked around. While I was relaxing in Honolulu, my company had moved to this new location. I felt like a bug under a microscope. I knew

that we had to have friendly observation posts on the hills surrounding us, and that made me feel a little bit safer—just a little
bit. The enemy probably had observation posts somewhere up
there, too.

"Hey, sir. Welcome back," called my Third Squad leader.
"How was Hawaii?"

"It was wonderful back in the world," I said. "Clean, beautiful, and nobody shooting at me. But it was cooler than I
expected."

"Still hot as you-know-what here. While you were gone we
had a visit by Tarzan."

"Who?"

"Tarzan, the guy on TV."

"No kidding? Why was he here?"

"Well, he went on patrol with First Platoon. Actually walked
with them. Not like the reporters that come here, stand around,
then go and write their 'firsthand combat stories.' He was a real
nice guy. Signed autographs, asked how we were doing, and just
shot the shit with us. He sure is a tall, skinny guy. He stayed
most of the afternoon."

"Sorry I missed it." I walked to my CP and dropped my gear.
Sergeant Mayer was sipping a cup of coffee and filled me in on
what had happened during the week I was gone.

"During a search and clear mission three days ago, Alpha and
Charlie companies discovered a large enemy base camp with a
hospital complex, training areas, and over 400 bunkers on a
ridgeline a few kilometers from here. The point man walked up
on it."

"What about the enemy? VC anywhere around?"

"Not the first day. We found lots of recoilless rocket rounds,
RPGs, B40 rockets, and AK-47 ammunition. There were four

fresh enemy graves. We had prepped the area with artillery first, so we did kill a few before we went in. We received mortar rounds from that vicinity the night before, so we knew the enemy was there. The others must have scattered when the artillery landed. They knew we were on the way."

"You said 'not the first day'?"

"Yeah. Charlie Company went back the next day. It got too dark the first day before we could finish clearing the area, so they went back. While they were destroying the bunkers, machine guns and AK47s opened up on them from a ridgeline above. When Charlie Company fired back, the enemy pulled out. They left several blood trails when they dragged their casualties into the jungle. C Company found a large hospital complex and all kinds of medical supplies. The whole area covered about a click and a half. It had to be a regimental base camp. They also found a lot of ammunition."

"Well, looks like I missed the excitement," I said.

"I'm sure you don't mind. You had your own excitement in Hawaii, right?"

"Guess I did. Well, Sergeant Mayer, I guess you are now officially an old timer in country."

"Yeah, I'm enough of an old timer to know that we need to get out of this hole in the ground. I'm not comfortable with all those hills around us. I feel like we're sitting on a bull's-eye."

"Me, too. Thankfully we've got a mission coming up. When I got off the chopper, the CO told me to report to the CP at 1000 for a briefing. Looks like we're going somewhere soon."

"Good deal, sir."

Later that morning I reported to the company CP and, along with the other two platoons, received my mission brief. On the map, the CO pointed to a streambed and wide ridgeline three kilometers away that my platoon was to reconnoiter. An LOH had received small-arms fire from that area late yesterday. Artillery had been called in, and now we had to go in and find out if anyone was there.

All preparations were finished by 1130. "Saddle up, First Platoon," I ordered. All squads reported they were ready to depart. "Point man, move out." Looking at my RTO, I said, "Once we're outside the perimeter wire and into the jungle, conduct a commo check with the company."

"Roger, sir."

We walked for about an hour without incident. The underbrush became heavy, and moving through it was difficult. We followed the stream for another fifteen minutes and the trees began to shade the sunlight. A single canopy of trees gave way to a double canopy, and the light became dimmer along the streambed. Fortunately, the brush thinned out and we could move easier and see farther ahead. I motioned for the squads to spread out and increase the interval between soldiers. That way, if the enemy fired on us it would be more difficult to hit more than one individual at a time. If we were bunched up, one round might hit two or three individuals, or one grenade could cause several casualties.

Specialist Marks, on point, signaled to halt and drop down. He had spotted something up ahead. I moved forward quietly to see what concerned him.

"Sir, I saw movement about fifty meters ahead just to the right of that large tree." He whispered as he pointed off to his right front. "Couldn't tell exactly what it was, but it moved fast down that trail. May have been one or two dinks. Hard to tell in these shadows."

"OK. I've been smelling dinks for a while. They must be in the area. Turk, hand me the radio handset." I paused then spoke into the radio quietly, "Six-One, this is One-Six. I've got movement to my front. Over."

"Roger, One-Six. Can you tell what it is? Over."

"Negative. My point thinks it was a couple of dinks but can't be sure in this light. They're definitely here. I can smell them."

"Roger. Continue to move forward. Give me your location and I'll have the mortars prepare to support, if needed."

I provided the grid coordinates and signaled for the platoon to move out again. Everyone was alert and looking all around in case the enemy waited for us ahead.

"One-Six, this is Two-One," the Second Squad leader called on the radio. "We have three camouflaged bunkers thirty meters off to our left flank." Again, I signaled for the platoon to halt.

"Roger, Two-One. Maintain your position. Do you see any movement around the bunkers?"

"Negative at this time."

"OK. Hold tight for the moment." Reaching for the company radio, I waved Sergeant Mayer up to my location. As he arrived, I called the company commander. "Six-One, this is One-Six. Over."

"This is Six-One. Over," the CO responded.

"This is One-Six. I've spotted three bunkers ahead and off to my left flank. Request permission to recon by fire. Over."

"Roger. One-Six. Proceed and keep me informed. Out."

Turning to Sergeant Mayer, I said, "Bring the squad leaders forward."

A few minutes later, all squad leaders were huddled around me. "All right, men, bring your squads on line quietly and let me know when all are in position. Make sure the M79 grenadiers drop their rounds seventy-five to one hundred meters ahead of us. Also, keep the M60 machine gunners with you. I don't want them to fire unless we receive fire. Tell the men to move out slowly on my signal and not to get in a hurry. Keep on line and don't let anyone get ahead. The signal will be a three round burst of fire from me. Each man fires one magazine unless we receive fire. I'll throw yellow smoke to signal ceasefire. Got it? Questions?" There were none, so they hustled off to inform the squads. Ahead, all was quiet.

Sergeant Mayer brought the squads on line and waved that all was ready. I slowly stood up and motioned for the platoon to get up. I took a deep breath and fired three quick rounds from my M16. Then the air exploded with the sounds of twenty M16s and the plop of M79 grenade launchers spitting forth their 40mm rounds. Seconds later, the grenade rounds impacted in the distance as the M16s continued to fire. Quickly reloading, the grenadiers fired again. One round fell short, about twenty meters ahead, and exploded in the mouth of a bunker to my right. Debris and shrapnel blew back in our direction and one grenadier grabbed his throat and fell to the ground.

"Medic! Medic! Shorter's hit," yelled a soldier to my immediate right.

"On the way!" Doc sprinted to the wounded man's side.

The firing slowed down. Apparently, whoever had been in the bunker complex had left. I threw a yellow smoke grenade and yelled, "Cease fire!"

"Sergeant Mayer, take the platoon and sweep through the complex. I'm going to check on Shorter."

I ran the short distance to Shorter. Doc was bending over Shorter, who was lying on his back. Doc was holding his head to the side and putting pressure on his neck. Blood covered Shorter's face and Doc's hands, bubbling up through the medic's fingers. Doc looked up at me and reached for my hand.

"LT, grab the artery here and keep pressure on it." I reached into the hole in Shorter's neck and felt the slippery vessel. I squeezed hard and the blood flow slowed.

I called over my shoulder, "Turk, get a dustoff here right away. Have Sergeant Mayer find a clearing to bring the chopper in. Fast!"

"Yes, sir!" He began calling the company CP on the radio as he rushed to find Sergeant Mayer.

Shorter was pale but still conscious. I continued to hold the blood vessel until Doc tied it off and applied a bandage. "Sir, we've got to get him out of here ASAP."

"Yeah, I know. We're working on it."

A moment later, Mayer walked up and motioned towards Shorter. "Sir, how's he doing?"

"He's hanging in there for now. What's the dustoff status?"

"The medevac is on the way; it'll be here any minute. I had the Second Squad clear a small landing pad about fifty meters up the trail. Looks like the VC scooted. We found one body in a bunker. Grenade or artillery must have got him. Also found some pieces of clothing, lots of blood trails, and some AK ammunition. They left in a hurry. We found some food and a rice pot over a fire—still cooking. We must have interrupted their dinner."

"Thanks, Sergeant Mayer. I hope Shorter makes it. Damned freak accident."

The medevac chopper arrived in a few minutes and we loaded Shorter onboard. He was weak but still alive. "Don't worry LT; he'll make it if the chopper gets him to the hospital quickly. Thanks for your help."

"Yeah. Thanks, Doc. Sergeant Mayer, let's destroy these bunkers and then get the hell out of here."

"WILCO."

17

CHU PA MOUNTAIN

February 1969

I FINISHED EATING a can of beef slices just as a call came over the radio. "One-Six Romeo, this is Six-One Romeo." My radio operator had a mouthful of sliced peaches, so he handed me the handset.

I answered the company commander's RTO, "Six-One Romeo, this is One-Six."

"Roger. Six-One requests your presence."

"On my way. Out." I put on my helmet, grabbed my M16, and headed toward the company CP. When I arrived, I saw that the other platoon leaders, the FO, and First Sergeant MacCardle were already seated.

Captain Shu, whose real name was Schlusser, pointed to a place near the fire. "Have a seat, One-Six." He was eating a C-ration and drinking a can of Coke. Tall and thin as he was, he

113

always seemed to be eating. We platoon leaders had a habit of taking our least popular C-rations, such delicacies as tuna loaf and fruitcake, to the CP, where Shu would open the cans and finish them off. I was amazed he could eat so much so often and still be so thin. We jokingly called him the human garbage disposal.

He put down his meal and said, "We've got a mission first thing in the morning."

I took my helmet off, flipped it upside down, sat in it, lit a cigarette, and started to heat a cup of coffee over the fire. Though we'd only been at this patrol base a couple of days, I was ready to move out. "Where're we going, sir?"

"Chu Pa Mountain, a few miles from here. B Company walked into a U-shaped ambush; they've been in contact over two days with at least two reinforced NVA companies—might be a whole battalion." He started opening another C-ration can. "The dinks are using six or seven machineguns, also B40 rockets. Bravo has some wounded and several KIAs; they haven't been able to recover some of the bodies." We all looked around at one another. Two days was a long time for bodies to be out in the hot sun. "Be prepared to move out no later than zero-eight-hundred. Arty and Spooky have been working the area pretty hard, but Bravo needs help. We're going in to get them out." I had seen the AC-130, affectionately called Spooky or Spectre, spraying its deadly accurate fire once before and knew that Charlie was catching hell. The 105mm canon fire mixed with 25mm or 40mm rounds made a fearsome, lethal combination.

He gave the grid coordinates, and then I pulled my map out of my pocket and looked at the area. The heavily wooded mountain's contour lines were very close together. This indicated steep slopes with ridges spreading out in every direction.

Walking would be rough and tactical movement almost impossible. I took a sip of coffee, thinking that we'd have to move in single file through the double and triple canopied forests—an ideal formation to get ambushed.

The captain took a gulp of Coke. "Charlie Company leads, we follow, Delta air assaults to the northwest of Bravo to clear NVA from the high ground." He pointed to his map. "Charlie moves to Bravo's location while we secure the high ground here and prepare an LZ to extract the dead and wounded. Have your medics in the first lift so we can send them forward fast. We'll land in a small clearing near the top of Chu Pa, then walk about a click west to prep a larger LZ for extraction." He set his Coke down and pulled a candy bar from his pocket, "First Platoon leads, then Third, then Second. I'll be behind First."

I listened to the rest of the FRAGO, then headed back to my platoon's area. I briefed the squad leaders and we began the business of setting up the night's security and preparing for the next morning's movement. Weapons were cleaned again, and Sergeant Mayer issued additional ammo and grenades. Resupply choppers started bringing in extra water, food, and ammo. I stole a few minutes to write a letter to my wife; maybe I could send it out with the choppers.

The early morning began as a beautiful sunny day. We set up to get on the choppers as soon as they arrived. Dog, my new medic, stood next to me. He had arrived in country a few weeks earlier. Most medics liked being called "Doc," but our doc preferred to be called "Dog." I never figured out why. His shaggy red hair, though, did remind me of a cocker spaniel whose coat needed combing. We all looked a bit shaggy after several weeks of patrolling and living in the bush. Dog was a cheerful guy, a bit crazy but good at his job. His hair and goofy smile would have been right at home on a college campus. I figured he had been the class clown back in high school. I looked over at him. "You good to go, Dog?"

He smiled, "Roger, sir, I'm good to go."

The first slick swooped down and landed. I motioned for my RTO, three other soldiers, and Dog to board it. We climbed in and secured ourselves for the ride to Chu Pa Mountain. A short time later, I looked down at the small one-ship LZ blasted clear by artillery rounds. Except for the LZ, the mountain was covered with a thick semi-closed canopy of hardwood trees and dense undergrowth. A light fog swirled around the chopper blades and green smoke drifted off through the hundred-foot trees that surrounded the clearing. I looked to the left of the chopper and noticed a narrow trail meandering west in the shadows under the triple canopy. Charlie Company was already following that trail enroute to relieve its ambushed sister company.

The company landed and formed up for our move to the area where we would establish an LZ closer to B Company. It was humid, but as we moved under the trees the heavy shade made it cooler and evening like; it was almost eerie. Throughout the morning, occasional patches of sunlight pierced through the trees contrasting with the dark shadows that seemed to oversee our movement as we hiked down the trail. The ground fell off steeply in places along the ridge and, loaded down as we were, the walking was difficult. Still, we all stayed alert. The enemy was nearby.

We finally reached an area that, even though it was slanted, was adequate as an LZ. Of course we'd have to cut down some of the larger trees and then set up an elevated landing pad. Captain Shu walked over to me. "One-Six, you get to build the pad.

Also, have your medic link up with the rest of the medics at Charlie Company's location to help with the casualties."

"Yes, sir. How long before we can bring in the medevacs?"

"Hopefully by tomorrow morning. It's going to take awhile to build the pad. Good news is, Charlie Company linked up with Bravo around noon. They'll start moving back toward us in the morning. See you later, One-Six."

"Roger, sir." I heard artillery fire landing and Cobra gunships firing in support of Bravo and Charlie. Bravo had been fighting for three days. I looked to the west and thought of the dead soldiers who had lain in the sun since the first day.

Platoon Sergeant Mayer walked up and broke my trance. "Don't tell me, we get to build the pad."

"Affirmative, Sergeant Mayer. Let's get cracking."

"Roger, sir."

Each squad started preparing their defensive positions while Sergeant Mayer supervised the work detail that had to build the pad. They cut down trees to clear the area and fashioned a log platform that would create somewhat of a level plane for the choppers to land on. The landings would still be a dangerous operation, but the dustoff pilots were good at their job. The dead and wounded would get extracted.

Work and perimeter security continued throughout the day and into the night. Long firing continued all night, and Spooky's tracers sprayed the area to our west. By morning, the pad was almost finished. I ate a quick breakfast of scrambled eggs and ham, picked up a few rejected C-rats from the soldiers ("Who the hell would eat this shit, sir?"), and walked to the company CP. Captain Shu took the cans and started opening one with his P-38. "Bravo's en route, One-Six. They should be here in an hour or so. Is the pad ready?"

"Affirmative, sir. The men are putting a few final touches on it."

"Good, good." He took a bite of the C-ration fruitcake. "They got their most seriously wounded out, but we have to assist with extracting the KIA. When they arrive, we'll send the dead out from here. We'll remain overnight, then return to the LZ we came in on and get picked up. We're going to a temporary patrol base for a couple days, then to LZ Mary Lou for refit and resupply."

"Sounds good, sir."

"Bye the way, I got another call from HQ. Brigade wants you reassigned to them as a liaison officer. I told them you were on patrol again."

"When do they want me?"

"Right away." He put down his food and looked at me. "You want to go? You've been in the bush for six months."

"No, sir. I want to stay with the platoon. We work well together."

"Yeah, well I can offer you the company XO job again. Brigade might settle for that and find some other lieutenant to be the liaison officer."

"Sir, like I said, I want to stay with the platoon in the field. Maybe in another two or three months I'll be ready for a staff job, but not now."

"OK, but if they want you bad enough they'll get you. For now, drive on and we'll see how it all works out."

The company RTO walked up. "Captain Shu, Bravo Company is fifteen minutes out. They'll be coming in from the southwest."

The captain looked toward the southwest. "OK, tell Third Platoon to be alert for friendlies entering our location. And inform battalion that we need those choppers now."

"Roger, sir." The RTO took a few steps away and made his calls.

The captain then turned to me, "Frank, have some of your men assist Bravo with the casualties."

"Roger, sir." I moved off to inform my platoon sergeant.

For the next few hours, choppers came in to drop off supplies and took off to extract the body bags of Bravo Company's dead. Because of the short takeoff area, the lead chopper pilot decided to sling load the bodies rather than load them inside the chopper. The extra weight of the bodies would make takeoffs extremely dangerous. I watched as a chopper dragged one body through the tops of the trees because it didn't get sufficient height before flying off. I listened to the cries and shouts of my men, all of us afraid that the chopper would need to drop the load in order to clear the trees. The chopper gained height, load intact, and headed toward Kontum. We all exhaled a sigh of relief.

I was about to make my rounds of the platoon area when Sergeant Mayer walked up. He looked down at the ground and said, "Sir, you need to come see Dog. He's in pretty bad shape."

"What happened? I didn't know we took any casualties."

"He's not wounded, sir. He knew one of the dead guys from Bravo Company, a friend of his."

I rushed over to my platoon CP. When I got there, I froze. Dog was bent over with his head in his hands, sobbing uncontrollably. I'd never seen Dog sad before. He was always clowning around and laughing. Seeing him like this stunned me. A couple of his friends were sitting next to him. They stared at the ground with tears in their eyes. I squatted next to my medic. "What happened, Dog?"

Dog kept crying and couldn't answer. Sergeant Mayer answered for him, "Dog found one of his friends, another medic from Bravo Company. He was killed three days ago." I nodded to Sergeant Mayer, looked back to Dog, and got a quick mental image of a dead soldier lying in the sun on the side of the mountain.

Dog finally spoke. "We, we came in-country together, planned to get together after Nam. He ... he didn't believe in war but wanted to do his part." Dog, still crying, looked up at me. "He was a great guy, sir. He didn't deserve this." Dog started shaking and cried even harder.

My eyes watered; I fought for something to say. I knew what it was like to lose a good friend. I walked to my rucksack and took out the quart of Jim Beam whiskey Lieutenant Jenkins, the Company XO, had given me earlier. Now it was needed. I poured some whiskey into a canteen cup and gave it to Dog. For the next two hours, Dog and I talked about friendship and about the plans he and his friend had talked about on the plane to Vietnam. Drafted, Dog's friend was deeply religious. He had been an Eagle Scout, college student, and Sunday school teacher from West Virginia. He couldn't wait to finish his year and return to his family. He refused to carry a weapon. As Dog talked and drank, I continued to refill his cup and listen. It was all I could do for him. Eventually he passed out.

We left the ghosts of Chu Pa Mountain behind us the next morning. We took our memories with us.

I didn't know the exact circumstances of Dog's friend's death then, and wouldn't know until thirty-five years later. Dog's friend was a remarkable person. On February 11, 1969, Company B moved in an assault on well-fortified enemy positions and became heavily engaged with the numerically superior enemy force. Five members of the company fell wounded in the initial assault. Under intense enemy fire, Dog's medic friend treated several wounded soldiers and began running toward another seriously wounded man. In attempting to save his fellow soldier, he was mortally wounded. During that fight, Private First Class Thomas Bennett earned the Medal of Honor. He is one of only two conscientious objectors ever to receive that honor and the only one during the war in Vietnam. He was also posthumously promoted to corporal.

Medal of Honor Award Citation
Private First Class Thomas Bennett

Cpl. Bennett distinguished himself while serving as a platoon medical aidman with the 2d Platoon, Company B, during a reconnaissance-in-force mission. On 9 February the platoon was moving to assist the 1st Platoon of Company D, which had run into a North Vietnamese ambush, when it became heavily engaged by the intense small arms, automatic weapons, mortar and rocket fire from a well fortified and numerically superior enemy unit. In the initial barrage of fire, 3 of the point members of the platoon fell wounded. Cpl. Bennett, with complete disregard for his safety, ran through the heavy fire to his fallen comrades, administered life-saving first aid under fire and then made repeated trips carrying the wounded men to positions of relative safety from which they would be medically evacuated from the battle position. He valiantly exposed himself to the heavy fire in order to retrieve the bodies of several personnel. Throughout the night and following day, Cpl. Bennett moved from position to position treating and comforting the several personnel who had suffered shrapnel and gunshot wounds. On 11 February, Company B again moved in an assault on the well-forti-fied enemy positions and became heavily engaged with the numerically superior enemy force. 5 members of the company fell wounded in the initial assault. Cpl. Bennett ran to their aid without regard to the heavy fire. He treated 1 wounded comrade and began running toward another seriously wounded man. Although the wounded man was located forward of the company position covered by heavy enemy grazing fire and Cpl. Bennett was warned that it was impossible to reach the position, he leaped forward with complete disregard for his safety to save his comrade's life. In attempting to save his fellow soldier, he was mortally wounded. Cpl. Bennett's undaunted concern for his comrades at the cost of his life were above and beyond the call of duty are in keeping with the highest traditions of the military service and reflect great credit upon himself, his unit, and the U.S. Army.

Some of Alpha Company's leaders. The company
commander is in the rear; at his left in the rear is the forward observer. Next row, left to right: the author, the
Second Platoon leader, the company executive officer,
acting first sergeant. Front: author's platoon sergeant.
(October 1968)

The author upon graduation from the Infantry Officers'
Candidate School at Fort Benning, Georgia.
(November 1967)

Company commander, forward observer, platoon leaders,
and executive officer. Author is in the rear middle.
(December 1968)

The author next to his hootch. This shelter was constructed by fastening two ponchos together and staking down the ends. A mosquito net was usually hung inside. The hootch was normally set up a few feet to the rear of the fighting bunker.

Platoon leader's radio telephone operator (RTO).
He maintained radio contact with the company and passed
any information from the platoon leader to the company
commander's RTO. He was a key individual in the platoon.
The platoon is preparing to load onto helicopters for the
move back into the bush, or jungle.

Smoke from a smoke grenade marks the location for the helicopters to land. This is the pickup zone, or PZ. Landing zones, or LZs, were also marked in this manner. Various colors were used: yellow, or "Barry Banana"; purple, or "Goofy Grape"; orange, or "Jolly Olly Orange"; and so on.

The platoon loads onto a CH-47 Chinook helicopter.
Smaller UH-1H "Huey" helicopters were used for shorter
trips or assaulting into hot LZs. The larger CH-47 could put
a whole platoon onto the ground at one time.

The author points out his location on his map. The fighting
bunker he's sitting on is hastily constructed and required
many more sandbags of dirt in order to provide protection
from incoming mortar rounds.

Waterhole at Polei Kleng. Near the Special Forces Camp,
this was a favorite wash site. Both vehicles and people got a
bath.

Polei Kleng waterhole was a favorite place to relax and clean up for US soldiers, civilians, and Vietnamese Special Forces soldiers. Note the woman washing her clothes in midstream.

The platoon sergeant hands out candy to the children near Polei Kleng. The mountain in the background was the site of fierce fighting a few months earlier.

Montagnard children from a tribe near Kontum. They were
shy but still curious about the friendly American soldiers,
who usually had treats to hand out.

Cleaned up and taking a short break, the author wears clean jungle fatigues brought to him by the company executive officer, or XO. The XO brought simple luxuries every week or so. Things like cigarettes, candy, clean clothes, and snacks made life a bit more comfortable.

The author on Chu Pa Mountain during one of the last missions with his platoon before reassignment to brigade headquarters.

A damaged Russian truck used by the NVA to transport
supplies on the Ho Chi Minh Trail. It was airlifted by
helicopter to the brigade base camp.

LZ Highlander Heights was home for the second half of the author's tour. Behind him is the small sandbagged tent he shared with another lieutenant. (May 1969)

18

LZ HIGHLANDER HEIGHTS

February 1969

THE LAST CHOPPER took off to the east as I joined Platoon Sergeant Mayer at the platoon command post. The men were scattered about, lying around on the ground and propped against their rucksacks. They looked exhausted after their grueling trek on Chu Pa the past three days. Some smoked, others were opening C-rations, and a few began writing letters. Mayer spoke to the Three Squad leaders. With his wind-burned face and sunken eyes, he looked tired too.

"OK, let your men relax while we're here at the brigade base camp. There's no need for digging in or posting LP/OPs. In a few minutes, we'll begin rotating squads to the shower point and hot chow will be here around 1700. Plan to remain overnight and chopper out at first light."

"Damn. Clean fatigues and hot chow. Any chance for a haircut, Sarge?" asked Sergeant Baker as he scratched his head.

"Yeah. Barbers are set up in tents near the shower point. Everyone will get a chance, and I want to see the tops of everyone's ears by the end of the day. Got it?"

The three muttered their agreement and grinned. Mayer was tough but fair. Since joining our platoon he had quickly earned their respect. None of the squad leaders dared argue with him. He resembled a big Teddy bear with a crew cut. At the moment, his sandy colored hair badly needed a barber's clippers, too.

"Now get your men organized and spread out. Just because we don't dig in doesn't mean that we get too lax. Charlie could still drop a few mortar rounds on us here." Turing to me, he said, "Sir, we're set up over here. I've got Harmon building a fire for hot coffee."

"OK. I think I'll catch a quick nap after that coffee." I said.

I heard a jeep pulling up and someone yelled out, "Where's First Platoon?"

I recognized that voice. The First Squad leader, Sergeant Baker, yelled back, "Over here."

Captain Trotter, the former Alpha Company commander, stood next to the jeep smoking as Captain Shu unfolded himself out of the back seat.

"Lieutenant Evans. Frank. Report over here," Trotter ordered. He had given up command of Alpha Company a couple of months ago to Captain Shu, and now he was the assistant brigade operations officer. A "staff wiener," as the field troops say.

As the two captains stood side by side, I noticed the striking contrast. Looking freshly scrubbed, Trotter was wearing tailored, clean fatigues with nametag and combat patches sewn on. His solid frame was built close to the ground. Tall and slender, Shu needed a bath, a haircut, and a clean uniform. Wearing dirty, ill-fitting jungle fatigues, he looked as if he had been living in the jungle for weeks on end, which in fact he had. Both were extremely competent commanders. I presumed Captain Trotter was equally competent as a staff officer. Trotter looked stern, while Shu's expression was like that of a kid caught smoking one of his father's prized cigars. The jig was up. Trotter knew that I wasn't on patrol now and I couldn't hide. *Damn.*

I reluctantly walked over and saluted. "Hi, sir. How's it going?"

Tossing his cigarette on the ground, Trotter said, "Lieutenant, grab your shit and throw it in the jeep. You've got a new home." He motioned up the hill towards the brigade operations center a hundred or so yards away.

"You know, sir, last time I heard you say something like that, you were firing Lieutenant Wood and giving me his job," I said.

"Consider this a move upstairs. Besides, I have had my last butt chewing from the brigade S3 for not bringing you to brigade headquarters weeks ago. You are now the brigade liaison officer assigned to the S3 shop. You now report to me."

"Frank, I tried to talk him out of it, but his orders from the brigade commander were to get you or not come back," protested Captain Shu.

"I can guess who recommended me for the job."

The corners of Trotter's mouth turned up in a smirk. "Well, I figured you had enough time in the bush, and we needed a halfway decent lieutenant, so … Besides how do hot chow, showers, and clean clothes sound?"

Grinning, I said, "Thanks for the halfway compliment, Captain. I'll trade the hot chow and all just to stay here for a few more weeks."

"No way. You are going back with me if I have to hogtie you. Colonel Nickle gave me a direct order to bring you back." Captain Trotter had also argued against being assigned a staff job two months ago and had lost that fight, so I knew it was useless to argue.

I walked over to the CP and picked up my rucksack and weapon. I turned to Sergeant Mayer. "Well, looks like the platoon is yours, Sergeant Mayer. I'm being kidnapped. Good luck." I handed over my watch, compass, flashlight, and two grenades. "Here, you'll need these more than I will."

Mayer handed the loot to Sergeant Baker and stuck out his hand. "Sir, it's been a pleasure. Best of luck. I'll say your goodbyes to the men, since it looks like the captain is in a hurry."

"Yes, we are, Sergeant. Shu, take care. I'll see you later. You'll get a replacement officer in a few days."

Shaking Trotter's hand, Shu said, "Thanks, Dick." He emphasized Trotter's first name and grinned. Looking at me, he said, "Frank, good luck. It was good working with you. Your platoon will do fine under Sergeant Mayer. They're squared away. Mayer, let's go get some chow."

I joined Captain Trotter in the jeep and headed for brigade headquarters. Leaning back in his seat and sticking a cigar in his mouth, he glanced at my faded, dirty uniform and said, "We'll get you cleaned up and fed before you meet the brigade commander. You look like you've just crawled out of the jungle."

Trotter jumped out of the jeep when we arrived at the brigade headquarters a few minutes later. Motioning toward a tent fifty yards away, he said, "You'll share that tent with Lieutenant

Parkins. Showers are over there behind the tents. Water's cold, but it'll still take off the jungle crud. We'll see about getting you some clean jungle fatigues and a haircut. Meet me in the operations center in about an hour."

The tent was a standard army "general purpose, small," or GP Small. It was encircled by sandbags stacked two deep and four feet high to provide some protection from small arms fire and shrapnel in case we got attacked while sleeping. Inside the tent were two army cots with mosquito nets hanging over each. I took the one with a folded blanket on top. The other cot had a pair of boots and shower shoes underneath, so I guessed it belonged to Lieutenant Parkins.

Not bad living conditions, I thought. I was about to become a REMF (rear echelon m***** f*****). That was what the field troops usually called the troops in the brigade and division firebases. Soldiers who sat out the war with supply or administrative non-combat related jobs had hot chow, cold beer, and latrines with showers. They were easily recognized by their clean jungle fatigues, with sewn-on name tapes and unit patches, and by their shined jungle boots. Combat troops saw these comforts only once or twice during a tour—when they first arrived in country or departed for the world.

As I began unpacking my rucksack, a bald lieutenant wearing Signal Corps sewn-on rank and insignia entered the tent. "You must be Lieutenant Evans. I'm Jerry Parkins." He extended his hand.

I shook it. "Frank Evans."

"Captain Trotter asked me to help you get some clean clothes and lunch before you go to the TOC. You can use some of my boot polish, too. The barber's tent is down the hill a little bit. I'll show you so you can get a haircut when you have a few minutes later."

"Thanks. Guess I look a little rugged. I've been in the bush for several months."

"That's what Captain Trotter said. He said you were one of his platoon leaders before he got bumped up to staff."

"Yeah, I just got hijacked by him a little while ago. Didn't even get to say so long to my men first."

"Well, Trotter has gotten a lot of pressure to get you here for the last couple of weeks."

I smiled. "Yeah, I heard. I've been avoiding the radio, and Captain Shu, Trotter's replacement in Alpha Company, has been helping me. We got caught when we came into the brigade base camp, so here I am." I looked at the mosquito net hanging over my bunk. "Are mosquitoes that bad here?"

"They can be, but actually the net helps keep the rats off. They can get pretty big here since the dump is just outside our defensive perimeter. Just make sure you tuck the net tightly under your air mattress at night."

I finished unpacking my belongings, took a shower, and made a mental note to buy some boot polish later at the small exchange tent I had seen as we drove in. Parkins and I went to the mess tent and got some chow.

Between bites of my thick baloney sandwich, I asked, "Where's the brigade TOC?"

"You've been walking all around it. See that guard in the small sandbagged bunker over there?"

"Yeah."

"Well that's the entrance to the underground TOC. He'll check you off on his access roster and let you inside. There's an emergency exit just over the hill a few yards. It's not used except in emergencies."

"Thanks. Guess I had better go on in."

"Yeah. I'll see you later tonight at dinner in the mess tent. The brigade commander wants all his officers to dine together every evening. Expect beef stew."

"Sounds OK to me."

Parkins laughed knowingly and walked away.

The rest of the day I met the staff, got an orientation on my duties, and tried to adjust my eyes to the dim light inside the TOC. My major tasks would be assisting the S3-Air Staff Officer in developing and scheduling airstrikes and coordinating the defense of the base camp. Also, I would be expected to maintain coordination with the local Special Forces headquarters. Each morning and evening I would fly a five-kilometer circle around the camp in a small observation helicopter with a pilot looking for any suspicious activity, such as enemy mortar positions or enemy troop movement.

Following the brigade tradition, I was invited to sit at the brigade commander's table as the newest officer on the staff. The one-course dinner that evening was served steaming hot in a large bowl. The stew was filled with lots of potatoes, carrots, and onions. Floating in the brown gravy were a few morsels of beef and tiny pools of grease or fat. Sliced loaves of bread were set on the table and I looked for the butter or margarine without success. Hot coffee and warm, reconstituted milk were served by the Vietnamese dining room orderlies.

Colonel Nickel, the brigade commander, said, "Well, Lieutenant, it's good that you could finally join us on the staff." I glanced at Captain Trotter, who nodded and grinned. Major Fielder, sitting next to Trotter, just scowled. He was a large man and looked as if he could have been a pro football lineman. I found out later that he was a former All-American tackle. He was all business—at least for now.

"Thanks, sir. I'm sure that I'll learn a lot here."

"How do you like the stew?" asked Colonel Nickel.

"Sir, it's a great change from the C-rations."

I gobbled it down. Most of the diners picked at their food, except for the brigade commander, who seemed to enjoy it. After dinner, cigars were passed around for those who smoked; then it was back to the TOC for a couple of hours of work before the night shift took over. I looked forward to a uninterrupted night's sleep. No walking the bunker line to make sure everyone was alert and no worrying about the LPs tonight. The brigade defensive perimeter was manned and the duty officer for the evening was in charge.

That evening I wrote a couple of letters and quickly settled in for six or seven hours of sleep. It was a typically cool evening and a poncho liner was all I needed for a blanket. My tent mate was working late. It didn't take long before I drifted off to sleep listening to the sounds of the power generator supplying electricity for the lights and communication radios used by the TOC's night staff.

Lying on my back, I slowly awoke feeling as though someone were holding my feet. I moved them and began to open my eyes, although I was very drowsy. It was still dark outside. I couldn't understand why my feet were weighted down and tried to lift them. Something moved on top of my feet. Instantly I was fully awake. Raising my head and looking down at my feet, in the dim moonlight I saw the largest rat that I had ever seen in my life. It was perched on its rear legs on top of my ankles and staring directly into my eyes. As large as a house cat, its mouth was open and its large, pointed teeth were bared in a snarl. I had felt fear before, but this was an entirely new level of fear.

Reacting on instinct, I rolled to the floor as the rat scrambled off and ran out the door of the tent. Thankfully, my newly issued .45 caliber pistol was out of reach or I would have filled the tent with flying bullets. Now sweating and short of breath, I realized that Lieutenant Parkins was sitting up holding a flashlight and looking intently at me. He saw me on the floor and assumed that I had fallen out of bed.

"Are you OK, Frank?"

The words came out slowly, "Y-Yes. I ... uh ... had a visitor in bed a minute ago. A large rat got in somehow." I got to my knees and finally sat on the bed. "The largest damned rat I ever saw, and he was looking me right in the eyes."

"Shit! Thank God you didn't get bitten—or did you?"

"No, no. I'm OK now. That's a hell of a way to wake up though. Guess I'll be OK in a minute or two."

I looked at the foot of my bed and saw that the mosquito netting had come loose. I would never make that mistake again. I securely tucked the netting back in and walked outside to smoke a cigarette, cupping it in my hands so the light wouldn't show. I finished the smoke and eventually got back in bed. After a long while, I went back to sleep.

19
TRI-BORDER

February 1969

THE BRIGADE AIR operations officer and my immediate supervisor, Captain Barron, spoke from the doorway of my small cramped office. "Lieutenant Evans, I've got a mission for you." Standing next to him was Captain Young in his flight suit.

"OK, sir. Hi, Captain Young. What's up?" I stood and looked at the Air Force officer. I was curious; although my daily routine kept me busy, I was thankful for the break in the monotony and hoping for some excitement. I was about to get plenty of that.

Young, our forward air controller, nodded. I knew him from the brigade's daily operational briefings and had listened to him over the radio as he flew over enemy targets in his small O1E Birddog airplane. From his low-level observation flight path he directed the jets, or *fast movers*, in their bombing and strafing runs. The FACs were lightly armed with rockets but, unfortunately, were good targets for the NVAs 12.7mm antiaircraft gunners. The FACs marked the targets for the jets with white phosphorous smoke rockets then quickly got out of the way as the F4s made their approach with their ordnance of 500-pound bombs, or "snake and nape" as we called their mixture of cannon fire and napalm.

Barron looked at the pile of papers I had spread on the folding field table I used as a desk. "Lieutenant, are you ready to go for a ride?"

"Hey, sir. You bet."

"Captain Young is on his way to the airstrip. I'll have him take you up for a firsthand view of how a FAC puts in an airstrike. Since you schedule pre-planned strikes, I thought you might like to see one from the air. I know you've seen airstrikes from the grunt's view, in the jungle."

"Yes, sir, I have. Actually, I've called in a couple. They're impressive—and effective."

"Here's a chance to get a new perspective. We have reports of some new NVA antiaircraft positions. He's going to locate them and put some ordnance on top of them."

"Sounds good to me. I'm ready for some excitement."

Young smiled. "I can guarantee that. Grab your pistol and let's go. Mission time is 1030 hours."

"I'll cover your duties while you're off flying around. Just make sure you get back. Colonel Nickel wants that report on the sapper attack on the engineer compound last Thursday," said Captain Barron.

"Thanks, sir. I've just about completed the report. I visited the compound yesterday. Classic sapper tactics." Captain

Young and I left the TOC and jumped in his waiting jeep. The driver sped off to the airstrip a few miles away, and shortly afterwards we pulled up next to a small tin building. Young said, "Wait here a few minutes. Just want to get the latest weather information and confirm the target area."

He returned and we walked to the small aircraft parked nearby. "This is a Cessna O2 Skymaster. The twin-engine, twin-tail boom O2 has greater endurance and a little more speed than the O1 Bird Dog I've been flying. It's low flying and slower moving than the jets, which makes it ideal for reconnaissance and spotter missions. It gets the job done. I have a great deal of respect for this aircraft. Climb aboard. You're in for a treat." Barron knew that I loved to fly and regretted not applying for flight school following officer candidate school. Occasionally I got to fly the light observation helicopter around the brigade base camp, when one of the junior pilots flew the bird. Captain Young and I took turns as a passenger in those twice-daily visual reconnaissance missions, which provided a nice break from the dim light and smothering atmosphere of the TOC.

Young, a highly qualified fighter pilot, performed his pre-flight checks and in a few moments we were airborne. "Looks like a good day for flying," he said. "I'd rather be doing this than almost anything else I can think of. Almost. I do enjoy flying an F-4."

"It sure beats humping through the jungle with sixty pounds on your back. I started out in Air Force ROTC at school and planned to fly."

"What happened?" he said.

"Not enough money for school and what little I did have was spent on partying instead of studies. I wasn't mature enough to be on my own at college, so I dropped out and joined the army a few months later."

"Well, you did OK. What's your plans after your tour here? A career in the army?"

"Not sure. I still don't know what I want to be when I grow up." I laughed. "I always said that I wanted to be a beach bum. That doesn't seem very exciting now. Maybe law enforcement."

"Well, I want to keep on doing this until I'm too old to zip up my flight suit. Hang on, I'm dropping down closer to the treetops."

We quickly lost altitude and the trees rushed by the cockpit in a blur. We flew like this for twenty minutes, and then Young said, "Let's climb back up to get a look around. We're close to the tri-border area and you can see parts of the Ho Chi Minh Trail to our west. You'll see a couple of our Special Forces camps ten clicks or so from the border. Those guys take a beating from the NVA artillery located in the hillsides just west of the Vietnam border."

As he spoke, I saw a small Montagnard village, and a couple of kilometers to the west was one of our Green Beret camps. I checked my map. "Is that Polei Kleng below us?" I asked.

"Yep. Sure is."

"I've been there a few times. It looks pretty vulnerable from up here. There's the 175mm howitzers just off the airstrip."

"Yeah. I guess you know that's one of the favorite targets of the NVA artillery. Same as a camp just north of here called Ben Het. East of Ben Het is Dak To. You should see both in few minutes."

As Captain Young predicted, I saw Dak To, and as we turned west I spotted Ben Het in the hills north of a long runway. "Our C-130s resupply Ben Het on that airstrip. Lately the pilots have been reporting small arms fire and mortars as they land. Sometimes they have to divert to Dak To, and the supplies are convoyed by truck to Ben Het. Those convoys get ambushed pretty regularly, so we fly above the Cobra gunships. We often get diverted from our pre-planned airstrikes to support an ambushed convoy. Charlie runs like hell when our F-4s come in."

"I can attest to that. I've seen the effects on the ground and even at a click away they're pretty awesome."

"Straight ahead is the tri-border: Laos, Cambodia, Vietnam. In those mountains west of the border are concrete AA emplacements and reinforced artillery bunkers. We bomb them day and night, but they're well protected. They fire their shells and then wheel their big guns back into the mountainside. Sometimes we get lucky and catch one outside. Unfortunately, we can't send ground troops across the borders to take them out. Politics."

"Hey, that looks like armored vehicle tracks on the dirt road down there."

"Sure is. The NVA have armored personnel carriers and tanks hidden in those mountains. They know we can't touch them there, and once in a while they run up close to the border and launch a few rounds at the camps, then scoot back into hiding. The only time they came across and attacked a SF camp was about a year ago. They overran that one. We retook it though."

"Yeah, I heard."

Captain Young spoke into his radio, then listened for a minute. "The F-4s are on station and now's my time to check out the target area. Keep a good lookout for AA positions, vehicles, or anything else that looks inviting. We have reports of several reconstructed AA positions along the border."

Suddenly tracers raced up toward us from the ground. Without hesitation, Young put the Cessna into a dive and banked sharply to the left. "Guess the reports were accurate," he said. He made a wide circle and climbed higher. Pointing, he said, "Keep looking over there. I think the AA position is just north of the road on the other side of that hill. There may be others. We're going to make sure before I bring in the heavy stuff."

I watched the area he had indicated, and as we flew low and fast over the hilltop I spotted an AA gun crew with a mounted heavy machine gun. We blew by fast and low so the gunners didn't have time to react. They appeared to shout and gestured wildly at us as we streaked by. We climbed high and Young spoke into his radio again. "The F-4s are ready and anxious to take the target out. Look around closely to see if there are any other AA sites we have to watch out for."

Here was the excitement I was looking for. "Roger."

We climbed higher and Young pointed out the jets a few miles away. They were waiting for the FAC to mark the target with smoke. "OK. Frank, we are going to climb high, dive fast, and lay some smoke right of top of that target. Then we are going to get the hell out of the way so the fast movers can do their thing. Ready?"

Before I could answer, the Cessna began a steep climb. Shortly after that, Young said, "Here comes the good part." He pushed forward on the controls while turning the wheel. The aircraft rolled to the right, and we began a rapid descent. For the first time, I experienced several seconds of weightlessness. The floating sensation was exhilarating, though it didn't last long enough for me. Young leveled the aircraft out and said, "Nice, huh? Here's hoping we shake them up before they get their sights on us."

He fired two rockets that impacted just short of the target. "Damn. Was hoping to save the bombs for the next target. Guess the F-4s will have to take these guys out." As we banked sharply to the west, I heard the jets screaming in behind us.

As we climbed, I heard two thunderous explosions, quickly followed by two more. The jets came around and made another run at the smoking target. "Let's check out the damage." We flew over the target area and saw three large craters. Mission accomplished. No sign of guns or enemy troops. Smoking debris lay around the holes in the ground. Young reported the bomb damage assessment to the fighter pilots. "Thunder 45, this is Elliot 11. Good BDA. Target destroyed. Thanks, guys."

We looked around for another fifteen minutes and the jets reported they needed to expend their payload and return to base. Unfortunately, we found no other targets for them except for deserted AA positions. Captain Young gave me a good view of a concrete and steel reinforced NVA artillery position. It was buttoned up, so there was no action there. Besides, it was on the wrong side of the border. We couldn't touch it for now. The jets unloaded their bombs on the trail network and unoccupied AA positions. At least the NVA would be kept busy rebuilding their fortifications.

I had plenty of excitement that day. Reluctantly, I returned to the brigade base camp, my cluttered field desk, and my report writing.

20
CHANGE IN MISSION

February 1969

CAPTAIN TROTTER WAS sitting at his small field table reviewing the previous night's staff duty journal. "Sir, you wanted to see me?" I asked.

"Yeah, Frank. How're those reports coming along?"

"OK, sir. I don't mind telling you though, I'm a bit tired of staff work."

"Me, too. You're lucky. We've got another mission for you. You know Lieutenant Dodge has been up north at a Special Forces Camp for the past couple of weeks?"

"Yes. I'm not exactly sure what he's doing, but I know he's been gone."

"Well, he's been reporting enemy activity around Ben Het and coordinating the fire support from our artillery units. There's been quite a bit of enemy movement up there in the

156

past two weeks, and air observers have spotted company-sized NVA units and even some vehicular traffic. He's getting short in country and we need to replace him. We have to have a liaison office there."

"OK. I'm ready to go. Just let me know when."

"First thing after breakfast tomorrow. In fifteen minutes I want you to report to the briefing room and Sergeant Bell will bring you up to date. Afterwards you can go to supply and draw whatever ammo and rations you'll need for the next week. If you stay longer than that, you can get resupplied there."

"WILCO."

I went back to my corner and small field desk. After I wrote a quick letter to my wife, I went next door to the briefing room. Sergeant Bell and Captain Trotter were already there.

"Grab a seat, Frank. Go ahead, Sergeant Bell," directed Captain Trotter.

Although he was showing his age now, Master Sergeant Bell spoke with confidence. He had been an infantry captain during the Korean conflict and reverted to his non-commissioned officer rank afterward, but he stayed in the army he loved.

"Lieutenant, on this map you can see where Ben Het Special Forces camp is located. Notice its proximity to Laos and Cambodia. Makes it ideal for infiltration into II Corps for NVA moving south. Highway 512 runs from the tri-border area in Vietnam through Ben Het and on to Dak To. At this location just inside the Vietnam border, there's an old French fort. There's been a lot of enemy activity near there in the past three weeks. The dirt road is good enough for both during this season. It's the only high-speed approach in the area. Trucks have been sighted in the vicinity, and aerial observers have reported numerous armored vehicle tracks along this portion of the road. The NVA have moved vehicles along the border."

Captain Trotter added, "Recently they brought more armored personnel carriers south into Laos and Cambodia. We haven't seen any on this side of the border yet. There's an NVA mechanized battalion reportedly based five kilometers inside Cambodia to the northwest of Ben Het."

Continuing, Sergeant Bell said, "Within the past week west of here, aerial observers have taken heavy machinegun and anti-aircraft fire. I understand you've flown over that area and seen some evidence of that."

"Yes. I did."

"Most of the fire is 37mm or .51-caliber machinegun. No missiles. Also, two nights ago at this location west of Ben Het, approximately forty to fifty flashlights were spotted moving east along a known trail network. Artillery and Spooky put rounds on the location and the lights went out. It appears that the NVA are moving toward Ben Het. Yesterday, a recon patrol near old Firebase Twenty-Nine encountered an estimated NVA company. Today Ben Het has taken over fifty rounds of incoming rocket and mortar fire."

"What kind of mortars?" I asked.

"A mixture of 82 and 120mm mortars combined with 75mm recoilless rifle fire and B40 rockets."

"Some pretty heavy stuff!"

"Well, they also have the capability of dropping 100 and 155mm artillery from across the border. There's also been some 122mm rocket fire recently."

Captain Trotter bummed a cigarette, lit it, and said, "Frank, we need you to tell us the extent of damage to the camp and to update us on enemy activity so we can assist if needed. Plan to be there for a few weeks. Major Stiever will be at Dak To. He will coordinate any support from there. Your reports will go to him and he will coordinate Air Force and ARVN support. Any questions?"

"No, sir. I guess it's going to be exciting up there."

"Guess so. Be careful. We'll support you with whatever you need. Now, you'd better go to the supply tent then pack your gear."

"Roger."

I left and prepared for my upcoming assignment. I looked forward to the change. Also, I would escape from the routine evening meal of beef stew, the colonel's favorite, which we had all come to expect and hate. Yes, back to C-rations and LRRPs.

21
SPECIAL FORCES CAMP A-244

February 1969

A S WE APPROACHED by Huey, the Green Beret camp looked like a small sand table model, except for the figures moving about and between the bunkers. I observed the surrounding terrain. To the west, I saw the rugged mountains of Laos and Cambodia approximately eight miles away. Over there the Ho Chi Minh Trail meandered from the north and was the main supply route for enemy troops and supplies coming south. Beyond the trail were the heavy mortar and artillery pieces used to strike Ben Het and other camps in the vicinity.

In between the camp and the tri-border area grew heavily forested jungles with double and triple canopies. The surrounding forests provided good cover and concealment for the North Vietnamese soldiers as they infiltrated south and brought food, ammunition, and medical supplies from North Vietnam by trucks, bicycles, and sometimes elephants. Numerous trails and paths crisscrossed through the forested rolling hills around Ben Het, and the network of trails provided the enemy foot soldiers easy access from their camps in Laos and Cambodia.

Below our inbound helicopter, unpaved Route 512 ran east and west from the borders. It circled south of Ben Het and ran east thirteen kilometers to Dak To. Although nearly impassable during the wet monsoon season, it was dry and dusty now. It was wide enough for trucks and armored vehicles and appeared recently used. The NVA had employed tanks with devastating success a year earlier at the Lang Vei Special Forces Camp near Khe San. We knew that they now had over one hundred armored vehicles, many of which were poised nearby in the protected staging areas across those borders to the west.

"Lieutenant," the co-pilot shouted over his shoulder, "get out fast once we land."

The door gunner explained over the noise of the wind, "They've been taking some pretty heavy incoming here. The helipad took some incoming mortar fire this morning and the supply chopper took some AK fire." I nodded and gave the thumbs-up signal. It would take me only a few seconds to get off the chopper, especially if someone was shooting at me.

The camp below showed signs of recent damage. It was divided into three small clusters of buildings and bunkers. Each sat on a rise in the terrain, and the main camp was located on the largest hill. The camps were connected by a perimeter of defensive bunkers and rows of triple concertina barbed wire, separated by ankle-high crisscrossed strands of barbed wire called tanglefoot. Several wooden buildings were scattered through the area and each was reinforced with sandbags stacked in layers against the outside walls. On the northern hill, I could see the US 105mm artillery pieces pointed to the west and three M-48 tanks positioned on the west hill.

From the chopper I could see activity in the camp below. Several indigenous soldiers moved from bunker to bunker, while a few cooked their meals over open fires. Near one bunker, a Montagnard woman was squatting with a small baby strapped to her back while she smoked a long wooden pipe. I learned that many soldiers lived with their families in the camp, which provided protection from the local Việt Cộng. Some had seen relatives or other males taken from their villages to serve as laborers or forced to fight in local VC units. Here they would be allowed to stay with their families in relative safety. Members of the Sadang tribe, these Montagnard soldiers just wanted to be left alone to live as hunters and gatherers, as they had for centuries. Not allowed that choice, they decided to serve here, where they could at least be with their families.

Flying at treetop level to prevent the NVA gunners from shooting us down, the chopper went in quickly to the northern edge of the airstrip. The downward rush of air from the blades raised a huge dust storm on the helipad. I grabbed my rucksack and bag then checked my .45-caliber pistol at my side. Everything was in place as I got ready to exit. We touched down and I jumped off, ducked my head, and ran towards the nearest bunker, where an unshaven, rumpled soldier waved me over to him.

"Welcome to Camp A 244, Lieutenant. I'm Sergeant Jones. That way to the TOC." He pointed up the hill to the north.

I turned to reply, but he was already en route to the chopper to pick up the duffle bag of mail that the door gunner had thrown to the ground. As he bent over to pick up the bag, the chopper lifted off and soared away to the southeast, leaving another whirlwind of yellow dust billowing behind it. I noticed several repairs in the helipad and some newer holes that remained to be filled in. They must have been the result of the recent enemy mortar rounds.

With the dust clinging to my sweat, I wiped my face with my neckerchief and started up the hill carrying the waterproof bag with my personal items. On my back, my protective gas mask and two canteens slapped against my rucksack with each step I took.

I looked around at the Special Forces camp. *So this is home for the next several weeks,* I thought.

22

BEN HET AND LOVIN' IT!

February 1969

CONSTANTLY UNDER ENEMY pressure, Ben Het had recently endured two probing attacks from the NVA that still trekked through the jungles around the camp. Mortar and artillery rounds impacted daily on the airstrip and the camp, pounding portions of this outpost into dust and debris. The evidence was all around: collapsed bunkers, splintered buildings, open craters. The daily enemy bombardment had decreased, although snipers periodically fired at the supply aircraft bringing needed food, water, and ammunition.

There were no trees or grass anywhere inside the camp's perimeter. The ground was dry and crumbled underfoot as I approached the tactical operations center or TOC. Here, daily operations were coordinated and communications were maintained with the local security patrols that searched the jungles and hills surrounding Ben Het. Nearby was the underground operations command post of the Vietnamese commander and his staff. Like the US command post, the South Vietnamese Special Forces' (LLDB) TOC coordinated ground operations and support, including bombing runs from the Vietnamese Air Force or VNAF fighter-bombers.

A major stood outside the entrance to the operations center. Assuming he was the camp commander, I started to salute, but then thought better about it and instead said, "Good morning, sir. Lieutenant Evans, Second Brigade, Fourth Infantry Division."

"Major Jake Snow, Fifth Group XO. Welcome to Ben Het, Lieutenant. Come with me. I'll take you to your radio operator."

We walked down the rough wooden steps into the darkened operations center, where I saw four more members of the SF team. Maps with colored grease pencil markings covered most of the walls, and the radios crackled with noise and communications from nearby patrols scouring the surrounding hills and trail networks. Everyone was busy at work attending to either the maps or radios. All of the team members were older than me, and although they were friendly enough, I was clearly an outsider. They all had that look that comes from enduring weeks of isolation and constant enemy pressure. It was an experienced but bone weary look. Even so, morale seemed good.

During the weeks ahead, I listened as they joked among themselves about their situation. Even though they had been under siege for several weeks, they had a motto in the camp: "Ben Het and lovin' it!" That phrase summed up the fearless resignation and wry humor of the men who occupied this small outpost overlooking the Ho Chi Minh Trail. Later I saw their motto prominently displayed above the makeshift bar in the teamhouse.

"Major Snow. Sir, we've got a unit in contact." A tall sergeant hurried over, glanced quickly at me, and then continued, "One of the recon units found an enemy camp with trenches and bunkers. They report one company of NVA and heavy automatic weapons fire."

"Any casualties?"

"Yeah. One friendly KIA and three wounded. Also, two US wounded. Medevac is on the way. Enemy casualties unknown at this time."

"OK. Sergeant Spence, take the lieutenant and show him his area of operations. I'll see you later, Evans." He hurried off to the command center.

The sergeant took me around the corner from the operations section. This was where I would operate the radios that provided communications with my brigade headquarters and the artillery fire direction centers.

"Stow your gear over there. I'll show you around in a bit," said the Green Beret sergeant. "This is Sergeant Smith, your radio operator."

A disheveled, light-haired buck sergeant sat at the radio. He had a bushy mustache. I was envious. "Lieutenant. Guess you replaced Lieutenant Dodge? He left on the resupply bird this morning. Took a few rounds of AK fire on the way out, too."

"Yes. I heard. No hits though." I said. "Quiet enough when I came in."

"Yes, sir. For now."

Smith was younger than I was by a couple of years. He was dirty and unshaven, wearing washed-out jungle fatigues with three stripes on his sleeves. No nametag showed, although he had a faded "US Army" nametape over his right pocket. My washed and pressed jungle fatigues contrasted with his. After becoming accustomed to laundry service and hot chow at my brigade headquarters, I must have looked like a recent arrival in Vietnam—or a REMF. His M16 rifle, ammo pouch, web gear, and gas mask hung on a nail next to the radios. A couple of fragmentary grenades hung from his gear, as did a red smoke grenade.

Sergeant Smith glanced at the combat infantryman badge above my left pocket. "Have a cup of coffee?" he asked.

"Sure," I said. "That would taste good right now."

"Help yourself over there." He pointed to the end of the wooden plank table. "Use my canteen cup. I've just been giving HQ the SITREP for today. You know, casualties, number of rounds of incoming, that sort of thing. Enemy activity has increased over the past few days. We took a shitload of incoming yesterday. The local security patrols have been running into small groups of NVA closer and closer to camp. So far, casualties have been light. Looks like they're testing our defenses."

"Yeah, I heard about the incoming," I said.

"It's kept us inside most of the day. The NVA must be registering their mortars again. So far today we took five rounds of 82mm mortar, ten 120mm rounds, and a B-40 rocket on the west hill. No sweat here though. Unless we get a direct hit, we're far enough underground to stay fairly safe. Gets pretty noisy though."

"How long you been in country, LT?" Smith asked.

"About six and a half months now. How about you?"

"I spent six months with an artillery battery and a couple months with the signal battalion at LZ Mary Lou. Been here three weeks. Duty's not bad. Cold beer, hot chow once a day, and plenty of sleep. You get accustomed to the incoming."

Sergeant Smith briefed me on our radio call signs and TOC procedures. As liaison officer to the Special Forces' detachment, my duties included planning and coordinating the artillery fire support for the defense of Ben Het as well as reporting enemy activity and keeping my headquarters informed of any requirements for additional support. Sergeant Smith would split the twenty-four-hour radio watch with me and help plan the fire support targets.

I stowed my belongings in the sleeping area in a separate underground bunker next to the TOC, then went to the briefing room, where a Green Beret sergeant briefed me on recent enemy activity and camp procedures. Sergeant First Class Spence confirmed that enemy activity had been increasing over the past several weeks. "We've had to cut back on our local security patrols so we can repair the damage from incoming. Our intelligence sources feel it's only a matter of time before the NVA attack," he observed. "If the NVA could overrun this outpost, they would score a major political victory. You know, create another Dien Bien Phu." He was referring to the Viet Minh's devastating victory that eventually drove the French forces out of Vietnam just fifteen years earlier.

"They want to humiliate US and South Vietnamese forces and demonstrate their strength. There are at least two NVA Infantry regiments across the border in Laos and more arriving every day. Add to that the reports of tanks and armored personnel carriers. You have probably already seen the mortar and artillery damage to our bunkers and the airstrip. Local intelligence sources reported that the NVA are prepared to commit large numbers of troops and equipment to the upcoming fight."

"How many personnel are here in the camp?"

"There's our SF detachment of four officers and six enlisted. You met Major Snow, who just recently joined us to coordinate operations from group. Then there's the arty gun crews and fire direction center—all total, around fifteen. Engineers have nine. Add to that the thirty-five Vietnamese LLDB and CIDG for a total of four hundred sixty-two."

"Most of the CIDG are Montagnards?"

"Yes. Over three hundred are from the Sadang tribe and around a hundred are Halang. There's a few Jea and Rongao. Oh, yeah. And one Chinese."

"Add Sergeant Smith and me for a total of thirty-seven Americans and close to five hundred ethic fighters, right?"

"That sounds about right. We're facing something over four thousand NVA in this area and just across the borders. Maybe more. We don't know how many other NVA units have infiltrated in the past several weeks."

"I've heard rumors of foreign advisors working with the NVA units. Anything to that?"

"We've been monitoring some of their radio traffic and our linguists have monitored radio transmissions in Russian. Our intel guys tell us that they probably have Russian advisors with them. That's close hold for now, so don't let that out." Spence stated that on one recent occasion, local striker units had seen two tall Caucasian soldiers fighting alongside NVA soldiers during a brief firefight about seven kilometers southwest of the camp. "A few days after that," Spence continued, "an unidentified helicopter was spotted flying back across the Cambodian border by a friendly aerial scout."

"Russian helicopter pilots?" I asked.

"That's my guess. Our patrols have discovered recently used landing zones near old Firebase 95, and it appears the NVA are using those helicopters to bring troops into the area. Probably recon and sappers," said Spence. "Newly constructed three and five-man bunkers and trenches were discovered on ridges here and here in the past two weeks," he said as he pointed on the map at former US firebase locations. "When the Fourth Division's First Brigade was relocated in December, they left their bunkers mostly intact. They left a lot of wire, too. Charlie has made good use of both."

He further explained that airborne scouts and forward air controllers had spotted enemy soldiers cutting down trees in nearby forests. The wood was used to provide flooring, shore up the walls, and reinforce the bunkers' overhead cover. This upsurge in recent enemy activity pointed to an enemy build up for a large offensive operation.

"The NVA are becoming bolder in their night movements, too. We've spotted as many as fifty flashlights and trail marking pots at night in several locations. That indicates the enemy is moving in large numbers."

Even more disturbing was the fact that on three occasions, splices into the camp's commo wire were discovered where the enemy had tapped into the defensive communications nets. Although patrols were assigned to follow the thin, black wire as it trailed off into the jungle, the wire ended seventy-five to one hundred meters inside the undergrowth. It appeared the enemy had been listening to the internal communications between bunkers.

After the briefing, I met the detachment commander, Captain French, who told Sergeant Spence to give me a walking tour of the camp. French reminded me to take my protective mask and weapon with me. "You never know when you might need them."

Walking out into the hot sunshine, Spence said, "We've been pretty lucky, and our casualties have been low. We lost four CIDG soldiers last week. Engineers had two soldiers killed and one wounded—all from incoming."

"I heard that you've had a couple of small ground attacks recently," I said.

"Yep, we had a firefight with an estimated squad-sized force on the west perimeter last week. We killed a couple of NVA. The northern hill took some AK fire day before yesterday. Because of all the enemy activity around here and on Route 512, truck convoys from Dak To were stopped. Too many mines and ambushes. Most of our supplies are brought in by air. The resupply birds take fire most of the time, 'specially the weekly C7–A Caribous and C-130s. They haven't been able to land for a while. Recently they've airdropped our supplies at night because of automatic weapons fire and incoming mortar rounds. Also, the NVA have begun to move 12.7mm antiaircraft guns closer to camp. Last airdrop missed the airstrip by 150 meters. Charlie got some of the supplies before we could get to them."

"I thought the enemy here were hardcore regular NVA troops," I said.

"Yeah, mostly. We have local VC units that operate with the main force NVA. As you know, they're regular army and they're better equipped than the VC. We know they have Russian trucks across the border in their camps. We've had reports of tanks and armored personnel carriers over there, too. Their artillery's located in Base Area 609 just west of here across the border."

I nodded. "Yeah. I've seen their concrete reinforced artillery and antiaircraft positions from the air. Our F-105s and F-4 Phantoms couldn't touch them. The NVA just roll their artillery back into the side of the mountains whenever we send in an airstrike. Their guns are mounted on rails and protected by metal blast doors. We need to put some B-52s in if we can ever get approval from Washington."

Flying into the camp, I had seen how it had been constructed around three distinct hills. Linked by concertina barbed wire, the defensive bunkers formed a common perimeter for better protection. The camp had been constructed a year earlier as a brigade firebase for the Fourth Division. A few miles away, on other hills, were smaller firebases that still showed the scars of the numerous battles for control of the area. After the US units had departed the area, the NVA and VC used these hills for short periods as bases from which to launch attacks on Ben Het, Dak Seang, and Dak To Special Forces camps.

The camp's defenses included a platoon of tanks, 105mm and 175mm howitzers, 4.2-inch or four-deuce mortars, 81mm mortars, machine guns, and quad fifty's (four synchronized .50-caliber machine guns on a single platform). They were placed so that they could support each other in the event of an attack. The 105mm artillery tubes could be lowered and fired in direct fire if needed. Their beehive rounds were extremely effective and very much feared by the NVA and VC. Placed in front of the bunkers were trip flares, command detonated 55-gallon drums of foogas, claymore mines, and simple alarms made by placing rocks into empty C-ration cans strung on commo wire. In addition, two Dusters were on the western perimeter of the camp.

"Well, LT, over there you can still see some of the enemy mortar and artillery damage from yesterday," said Spence as he pointed to four soldiers filling sandbags and rebuilding a small bunker.

"I see you have some engineers here."

"Yeah, their bulldozer comes in handy. By the way, over there in front of those two bunkers, we discovered cuts in the concertina wire. We check the wire every morning. Major Snow thinks the NVA sappers are trying to provide lanes for the next attack."

As we continued to walk, Spence continued, "It's also possible some of the cuts are being made from inside the perimeter. We probably have a few VC infiltrators in our CIDG units. Anyway, we've got that area covered with claymores and trip flares pretty good now. We have to check the claymores each morning, too, make sure they haven't been turned around toward the perimeter at night."

"So you think you have VC inside the perimeter?" I asked.

"Yeah. We picked up some new recruits a couple of weeks ago to replace the deserters. It's possible that a couple of VC infiltrators were in the group. It's happened before," Spence stated. "Also, someone's been tampering with our four-deuce mortar elevation and deflection settings during the night. That started about the same time we got those recruits. Haven't caught anyone yet. Captain Vahn, the Vietnamese camp commander, will deal with them pretty harshly if we do."

"Do you think the main attack will come from the area where the wire was cut?" I asked.

"No. We think that a diversionary attack will come from there, but the main attack will likely come from across the airstrip and Route 512 to the southwest."

We continued walking. I looked in the direction he was pointing and wondered, *When?*

23

INCOMING!

February 1969

T HE SOUNDS AND vibrations of the mortar rounds impacting were interrupted by yelling. "More rounds on the way," said Sergeant Smith. I prepared for more impacts and the loud thumps overhead. Fortunately we were protected underground and felt only the reverberations.

As any combat veteran of enemy mortar or artillery attacks can tell you, when you hear the word "Incoming!" that one word grabs your attention and produces an immediate response. Whether diving for a bunker or some other available cover, combat veterans don't hesitate to take immediate action.

While assigned to Camp A-244, I had many occasions to head for immediate cover. My months as a rifle platoon leader with the Fourth Division had prepared me well for many combat survival skills, including, when necessary, seeking overhead cover from VC or NVA indirect mortar attacks.

I quickly became accustomed to a daily routine of rising early, washing up and shaving, and eating a C-ration breakfast before relieving Smith from his radio duties. As he had told me earlier, you become used to the daily incoming rounds. *Used to them,* but not complacent about them. Each day's routine was interrupted with the impact of mortar and artillery rounds and the anticipation kept us on our toes.

Although there was no pattern to when the rounds came during the day, we knew that we could just about count on having our lunch inside the bunkers while explosions rocked the terrain above. A frequent guest during lunch (and at any other times we were receiving incoming rounds) was a large, playful cur that shared our bunkers' safe refuge. The scraggly mutt had somehow escaped the cooking pots of our allies and attached herself to the American soldiers assigned to Ben Het.

As SSG Bradley told me, "Whore is safer with us. She gets good food and knows she won't get eaten for dinner." She was tagged with that name because it aptly described her apparent promiscuity, evidenced by her constant state of pregnancy. I can't recall ever seeing puppies (which I assumed found their way into cooking pots) and often wondered where the father of her offspring came from. During my time there I never saw another dog in camp, male or otherwise. Perhaps the local VC had their own mascot that visited our camp early in the morning. We knew that some VC units sent large dogs ahead of their troops to set off mines.

We tolerated Whore in our camp mainly because of her ability to hear and react quickly to the artillery rounds from those NVA concrete bunkers to the west. Whenever artillery rounds were fired from those bunkers, Whore's ears would go straight up, her head would raise, and she became a blur of fur heading for the nearest covered location. Her keen ears picked up the sounds of those guns firing several seconds before any human ear could.

Whenever Whore wasn't nearby, we had to listen keenly for the first screaming inbound round, which then erupted in a loud explosion. We would scurry for cover as more rounds impacted. By that time, Whore was safely tucked away in the command bunker or under a makeshift bunk in the sleeping quarters.

I was amazed at the ingenuity of the Green Beret advisors, who devised small comforts to ease their stay on those exposed hilltops near the Ho Chi Minh Trail. Their teamhouse included a small "club" with a bar and cold beer. Although neither underground nor even adequately sandbagged, this small building provided evenings of limited relaxation, with cold Ba Muy Ba or Bier LaRue. Sometimes hot meals were prepared there as a reprieve from the constant fare of C-rations or the freeze-dried LRRPs. Just outside the club was a "one-holer" for the additional comfort of those assigned. Recognizable for it's typical construction, the outdoor facility was situated on a little bare knoll about thirty feet from the rear entrance of the sleeping bunker. At night, it was peaceful to just sit and observe the stars through the cracks in the plank door while taking care of business. As they say, almost heaven.

On this hot and sweaty morning, I was perched on the hand-crafted seat in the one-holer while taking care of business. Relaxing with a copy of *Stars and Stripes* in my hands and reading about some lucky airman's views on R&R in Australia at Queen's Cross, I felt removed for a few minutes from the hilltop near the tri-border. I glanced at Whore through the cracks in the door as she dosed in the dust outside and enjoyed the rays of the hot sunshine.

Suddenly, Whore raised her head and pointed her ears skyward. Although I heard no indication of incoming artillery rounds, Whore was up on her feet and streaking for the nearest entrance to the sleeping bunker.

I didn't hesitate either. I burst through the plank door of the outhouse with pants down around my ankles and scrambled for the same hole in the ground that Whore had just disappeared into. I dove down the dirt steps just as rounds landed near the team house.

Two of the Special Forces Sergeants, the SF radio night crew, had been napping in their bunks and looked up as I dove through the door while trying to pull up my pants. They began laughing even as the rounds began to impact above us. I didn't see the humor in my near death-experience at the time, but we later had a good laugh about it over a cold Tiger Beer. *Ben Het and Lovin' It!* became my motto, too.

Over the next several hours, Ben Het literally took a beating. Mortar rounds, 100 and 105mm artillery, 122mm rockets, and 75mm recoilless rifle fire smothered the camp. Prior to that day, thirty or forty rounds daily was the usual rate. This was definitely out of the ordinary! We counted over three hundred rounds of various types and size that hit all three hills. The main camp took most of the impacts. Everyone was expecting a ground attack to follow, but none developed.

"LT, they are either softening us up for more later or keeping us under cover so they can move troops closer in." Sergeant Smith's reasoning made good sense.

During that shelling period, one of the initial rounds obliterated the team outhouse. Quite literally, Whore had saved my rear end. When I fed her a special reward of C-ration ham and lima beans that night, Sergeant Smith said, "Hey, sir. You've made a friend for life now. She'll look you up every night at mealtime."

A week later on a nearby hilltop, an NVA artillery lieutenant was killed by a friendly patrol from Ben Het. Discovered in his shirt, wrapped in a cloth, was his journal with details on the dates, times, type, and number of aircraft flights in and out of Ben Het, the type of cargo the aircraft carried, the number of personnel departing and arriving, and notes on damage to the SF camp. His mission was to observe our activity and direct artillery rounds on our camp. I couldn't help wondering if he was watching that day, grinning with pleasure as I casually strolled to the outhouse and then calling in the artillery fire mission to interrupt my few minutes of solitude.

Thanks again, Whore.

24

SIEGE

February-March 1969

B EN HET WAS under siege. Each day, a deadly flurry of artillery and mortar rounds destroyed bunkers and damaged equipment. Casualties increased. Small-scale ground attacks tested the defenses of the camp. Friendly patrols near the camp encountered enemy soldiers in groups of five to ten men daily. Frequently, larger enemy units operated near the camp. On a recent mission, a mobile strike force unit reported battling an entrenched battalion-sized force of at least two hundred. Convoys were ambushed regularly. Aircraft received ground fire at every attempt to land. Helicopters, and occasionally a C-130 or C-7A, dared to brave the machinegun and mortar fires on the airstrip to bring in supplies. Our radio communication with the tactical command post in Dak To kept them informed about how defenses were holding up here.

I began to appreciate the comparison that Sergeant Spence made between the French garrison at Dien Bien Phu and Ben Het. Morale was high in spite of the constant barrage of enemy fires. Internal exchanges also relied upon radio, the least secure means of communication since the enemy could easily intercept them with a radio and the right frequency. We had to assume our conversations were being monitored; intermittently, an unknown radio station attempted to obtain friendly information on the location of patrols and their activities. The more secure field telephone landline wire was repeatedly cut by the constant bombardment or by saboteurs.

Sergeant Smith picked up the radio log and asked, "Anything goin' on this morning, sir?"

"We had one CIDG KIA on the west hill last night. One of the MSF units lost two KIA and two WIA, plus two US WIA. One was pretty badly wounded. They ran into bad guys in bunkers and took heavy automatic weapons fire. They're still in contact. Enemy has claymore mines, too."

"Uh huh. Must've captured some of our claymores somewhere. I tell you, sir. The enemy's moving all over the place around here. They're gettin' bolder."

"We have two MSF companies reinforcing us plus the one here in the camp. Another one has been requested from Dak Pek to reinforce the MSF company in contact now. Spooky has been working the hills and trail networks."

"I heard it. Three Gatling guns. Man, six thousand rounds per minute each! Sorta sounds like *hmmmmmmmm … hmmmmmmmm … hmmmmmmmm*. Those guns are spewing out red tracers every fifth round, but it looks like a steady stream of red lines from the aircraft to the ground. No wonder Charlie is afraid of the Dragon.

It was ironic to me that the much feared jungle-camouflaged AC-47, "Puff the Magic Dragon" as Spooky was sometimes called, used the same airframe that pulled WWII gliders into combat: a glider like the one flown by my namesake at Normandy in June 1944. The NVA and VC were cautioned not to attack the Dragon lest they infuriate the monster and bring down a rain of fire.

Sergeant Smith paused to conduct a radio check with Dak To and then continued, "Charlie's getting ready for a big attack. Looks like the start of the spring offensive. Polei Kleng and Dak Pek have had recent enemy activity."

"Well, our final protective fires are laid in. So are other pre-planned concentrations on likely targets. Plus, we've been shooting harassing and interdicting fires every day and night. That may slow down their vehicle movement at night. Oh, yeah. A tank platoon is joining us from Dak To sometime today."

"Good news."

"Yep, but they attract rockets, too."

"Just the same, I'm glad they're coming."

"Me, too."

"Late yesterday one of the FACs, Cider 21, reported tracked vehicles hidden under some trees west of here. Some kind of vehicle park, probably a staging area. Airstrikes and Spooky worked them over, but they limped back to the border. We're getting lots of support, but I agree things will bust loose soon."

"Yeah. Those 82mm mortars are tearing things up. You know the team house took two direct hits yesterday."

"Yep, but the bar's still intact. Also, there's still cold beer. Got to keep everything in perspective."

Suddenly I heard loud radio traffic and excited voices coming from the SF radios around the corner in the operations cell.

"Check out all that activity with the SF radios. Something's happening. I hear firing outside, too."

"Roger, sir."

Smith came back minutes later and reported that the West Hill was taking automatic weapons fire. "They spotted five NVA dressed in khaki uniforms and took them under fire. Cobra gun ships just arrived on station, too." I could hear the impacts of more incoming 82mm mortar rounds as he reported to me.

"Small ground attack. Probably probing our defenses. Too small to be much else. Cobras will take care of them."

I agreed. "There's been a lot of that going on. Guess they're looking for weak spots in our perimeter and seeing how close they can move in before being spotted."

"Just found out that the MSF company from Dak Pek couldn't get in to the LZ to reinforce the other company. The LZ was hot so they've been diverted here and will have to hump out. They should be landing on the airstrip shortly. Artillery preparation and gunships are working over the wood line near the airstrip to clear snipers and rocket positions." Smith poured himself a cup of coffee and said, "By the way, you know that CIDG soldier killed last night on west hill?"

"Yeah, sorry to hear that."

"Don't be. Just heard he was carrying VC identity papers from some artillery unit. I wonder how many other VC we have in the camp. Ironic that his own artillery killed him."

Throughout the remainder of the day, all three hills took more incoming mortar and artillery rounds. Losses included two water trailers, a 4.2-inch mortar radio antenna, several bunkers, and of course more casualties: one Montagnard child KIA, one Montagnard adult WIA, and two US WIA.

That evening, Sergeant Smith and I were checking grid coordinates against artillery targets numbers when we overheard on the radio that Spooky spotted an unidentified helicopter west of Ben Het moving toward the border. Minutes later, a local patrol also reported a chopper passing directly overhead. They said its engine sounded strange, not like one of ours.

Sergeant Smith looked up from the map and said, "Maybe those staff wieners will believe us now that the NVA are using helicopters. The guys on the West Hill shot at one with their .50-caliber machine guns about a week ago. Damned REMFs said we were seeing things. Unfortunately it escaped back across the border."

Sergeant Spence came bursting in and said, "Hey, sir, we've got flashlights on the outer perimeter on West Hill. How about cranking up some artillery right here." He pointed on the map at one of our preplanned targets.

"Can do." I was already reaching for the radio. "Fire mission," I called. The voice on the other end of the radio responded and I gave the target number. Within two minutes, rounds were on the way.

Spence called around the corner to me, "Good. Drop five zero and fire for effect."

I relayed the fire command to the fire direction center on the radio, and shortly I heard, "Shot out." Seconds later, I could hear the rounds impacting near the West Hill.

Spence said, "Good. The lieutenant on West Hill said the lights are moving. Add one zero zero and fire again." Six more rounds impacted. "Right on target. End of mission. The lights are gone and the .50-caliber machineguns are raking the area now. If anything's left, it ain't alive."

25

INFILTRATION

February 1969

I WAS SIPPING my second cup of strong, iodine-tasting C-ration coffee when Sergeant Smith came in carrying some mail.

"Here you go, sir. Letter from your wife. Spence told me that the C-130 dropped eight bundles of ammo off the west end of the airstrip and Charlie tried to get them."

Putting my letter away for the moment, I said, "Yeah, only four hit the strip and the rest went in the trees. Spooky worked the area over, but there's still a lot of ground fog out there. It doesn't lift until around nine thirty. There's a patrol going out to recover the lost bundles and check for bodies. Doubt they'll find anything but blood trails."

"You know that's where the security patrol found those new bunkers yesterday. Charlie's been spotted down there several times. That's where those rockets came from, too. I hope Spooky tore them up."

Muffled thumps indicated more incoming rounds landing nearby. I counted six this time. Suddenly a loud explosion at the entrance of the command post threw dirt and black smoke inside. Yells and curses filled the air along with the dust.

"Damn, that was too close. Everybody OK?" asked Captain French.

"Yeah. Just got dirt and shit all over my radio," said Sergeant Spence.

No injuries were reported, although everyone was a bit shaken up. I poured out the remainder of my coffee, which now had a film of dust floating on top. I reached for the letter in my pocket and found a quiet place to read. *Better read it while I can. It might get busy in a while.*

Over the next four days, lights were spotted on three occasions, which indicated the NVA units were positioning for an attack. Using a starlight scope, one artilleryman observed trail-marking pots that the NVA used to guide nighttime movement. A fire mission was called on the location. The pots were extinguished.

The West Hill withstood several small ground-probing attacks in addition to the ever-present mortar attacks. An inbound C-7A received automatic weapons fire while on final approach; it damaged and had be lifted out by helicopter. At 2045 on February 27, fifteen NVA were spotted running across the airstrip. The tank platoon on the West Hill fired their .50-caliber machine guns. A few minutes later, the West Hill took several rounds of AK-47 fire. The FACs received automatic weapons fire daily as they flew over enemy troops. The NVA were becoming more daring and aggressive each day.

A large enemy convoy was spotted moving at night on Route 512 toward Ben Het by an aerial observer. The report came over the radio.

Sergeant Smith said, "I can't believe these guys are moving with their headlights turned on! That's some brass." Again Spooky took them under fire, destroying several and damaging several more before they retreated to safety across the border.

Our friendly artillery gave as good as we got. Our 175mm and 105mm howitzers joined with Spooky and the Dusters to throw ordnance at every target the NVA presented. We could only estimate the vast number of casualties they were taking in their exposed positions. The NVA mortar, rocket and artillery fire were answered by our own mortars, artillery, gunships, tank fire, and airstrikes. Eight B52 strikes were flown between Ben Het and the border during this time. Still, the enemy continued to move closer and routinely approached the outer perimeter wire, where the CIDG machine gunners, M79 grenadiers, and 60mm and 4.2-inch mortars engaged them. It was obvious that the enemy was conducting a thorough reconnaissance of the camp's defenses.

The Special Forces duty sergeant kept a count of the number of incoming rounds each day. The number peaked at 308 on February 28. A shell analysis report from Saigon of the artillery fragments and fuses picked up on Ben Het's Main Camp confirmed that the NVA used a Soviet 85mm gun with a range of 15,650 meters. One such gun was observed by a FAC. The gun fired four rounds and retreated into its concrete and steel-reinforced bunker before fires could be called in on it.

As the number of incoming rounds decreased during the period between the end of February and the second day of March, intelligence analysts offered several possible reasons, from "The NVA have given up" to "The NVA are conducting planning, reconnaissance, rehearsals, and maintenance in preparation for the main attack." No one believed they had given up, so the latter scenario was the most likely. Ground contact with the camp also lessened; however, the movement of large troop concentrations continued. Charlie was still in the area and in large numbers.

I was lighting a cigarette when I heard the urgent call for a dustoff on the SF radio. I had heard the muffled explosions of more incoming rounds hitting the West Hill and shrugged them off as more harassment from the NVA. The number of rounds had diminished, and it was relatively quiet except for the occasional explosion that reminded us to stay alert. Sergeant Smith moved closer to the SF radio so he could hear the details.

"Sir, one of our tanks took a rocket round, wounding five tankers. One of them was the platoon leader. He's got a head wound; they've called for a medevac along with two other tankers."

We were still taking casualties, and although there was an uneasy lull in the enemy's artillery and mortar attacks, Charlie had a few other surprises for us. The West Hill took seven rounds of white phosphorus, or "Willy Pete," rounds. These deadly rounds caused white-hot burning of supplies and personnel. If a spot of phosphorus landed on an arm or face, the only way to remove it and relieve the burning flesh was to cut it out. Water would not extinguish the burning chemical.

The West Hill continually received small arms and recoilless rifle fire. Another ten rounds of incoming mortar fire announced lunchtime. In spite of the incoming and the sightings of three NVA near the West Hill perimeter, a C-7A arrived and unloaded the emergency resupply of mortar ammunition, rice, and water. Gunships were on station prepared to engage any enemy observed around the airstrip. Fortunately, the resupply mission was uneventful.

That evening after the supplies were unloaded, I heard our tanks firing from the West Hill. Sergeant Spence said, "Spooky's spotted heavy enemy movement on Route 512 west of here and a bunch of lights. There they go again! Those little bastards keep using their lights. They've got to know we are going to shoot the shit out of them, but they keep on coming!"

Spooky, artillery, tanks, and the dusters again poured on the firepower. Another enemy recoilless rocket was fired from the west end of the airstrip later that evening. Tanker machine guns fired back and reported a secondary explosion. Scratch one more enemy gunner.

I stood outside the bunker and watched as Spooky dropped flares west of the airstrip. The light created an eerie false daylight, with dark shadows that formed odd shapes as the flares drifted down. When they slowly burned out, I headed back into the TOC to send my SITREP to my headquarters. I heard the tanks firing again. The outgoing sounds of the tanks' main guns firing were reassuring although Charlie was undoubtedly plotting the exact locations of those tanks. If they weren't relocated soon, Charlie would zero his B40 rocket fire directly at them.

26
ENEMY TANKS

March 1969

THE RADIO CRACKLED and an excited voice reported, "This is Bravo Twenty-one. We've got tracked vehicle noises coming from the west. Estimate a thousand meters away. Over."

From the West Hill, the Green Beret lieutenant heard engines and rumbling sounds from multiple locations. He called for artillery and Spooky on the suspected location. Two patrols near the camp reported that they too heard the vehicle sounds and spotted over one hundred enemy ground troops moving along the trails. All the lights and vehicle sightings to our west meant that the NVA were poised for a major ground attack.

I was listening to the radio conversations intently. Earlier that afternoon, on the west side of the West Hill, a work party completed repairing the holes in the wire. The holes were caused by enemy sappers using bangalore torpedoes sometime in the night. Those explosions were masked by the incoming mortar rounds. About the same time, southwest of the camp, Cobra gunships and airstrikes supported a CIDG company in contact with an estimated battalion sized NVA unit.

"This is Bravo 21. Sounds like vehicles warming their engines and charging their batteries. Over."

Sergeant Spence yelled over the noise in the command post. "Hey, sir. Just got a report from Spooky that he's spotted another unidentified helicopter east of our patrol's location. The chopper is scootin' fast, back to the border." Spence paused and then reported, "That patrol is surrounded, and our tanks are supporting by fire. Spooky is adjusting fire."

"Alpha Six, we're still taking incoming and we've got enemy movement north of West Hill. We're engaging with machine-guns. One of our tanks is supporting with its main gun. Request artillery on preplanned targets. Over."

Reaching over my shoulder, Major Snow pointed on my map where he wanted the artillery to fire. "Put it here and here on these target locations. Let me know when it's on the way. In the meantime, I'm cranking up the four deuce mortars to start pumping rounds out there now." In the distance, we could already hear the dusters firing from the West Hill.

"Roger."

Sergeant Smith called the target numbers to me as I grabbed the radio handset and spoke into it. "Redleg Four-Zero, this is Lima Six-Three. Fire Mission. Vehicles and troops in the open. Over." I gave the target numbers and waited. Seconds later I heard, "Lima Six-One. Shot out, over." That meant rounds were on the way.

Seconds later, *Splash*. The rounds had impacted.

"Evans, adjust fire. Drop two zero zero and fire for effect," called Major Snow.

"Roger." I relayed the call to the fire direction center. "Lima Six-Three, drop two zero zero and fire for effect. Over."

The artillery worked over the area with 105mm rounds and we all hoped that they connected with the targets in the dark. The explosions to our west sounded fierce. We hoped they were as effective. Time was around 8:30 in the evening. Once again, a flare ship was dropping flares in hopes of highlighting the enemy troops and vehicles. Unfortunately, those flares also outlined our own positions to the enemy.

"Sir, I overheard Sergeant Spence saying the ammo bunker took a direct hit and it's on fire and shit's blowing up all over the place!"

"Yeah, I can hear it. Heard the supply room's on fire, too."

Major Snow again pointed to my map. "We just got confirmation of approximately twelve enemy vehicles, tanks included, moving on Route 512 ... here. Fire those targets ASAP."

"WILCO." I called in the new target locations and added, "Fire for effect." The 105mm artillery battery began throwing rounds all around the location that Snow indicated.

Just then, three artillery rounds hit outside the bunker and the shockwaves again scattered dust and debris all over. The dust in the air gave everything a reddish haze and it took extra effort to suck in the thick air. A faint but pungent, acrid odor accompanied the dust. I had smelled that harsh odor a few times previously. It was probably the stockpiled tear gas grenades from the ammo bunker explosions.

"Son of a bitch!" a voice yelled. "Tankers report that one of our tanks took a direct hit. Two killed, two wounded. The tank CO is hurt bad. They think it was a B-40 rocket."

"We're going to need dust off as soon as we can get one in," said Captain French. "Unfortunately it's going to be awhile."

I kept busy passing on our situation to headquarters and calling for fires. Sergeant Smith kept feeding me information from the SF side of the TOC.

"West Hill reports wheeled and tracked vehicles moving to the south and southwest of their location, LT. They estimate seven tracked and five wheeled vehicles approaching the camp." Sergeant Smith began to look concerned.

"Our tanks and dusters are throwing rounds out as fast as they can," I said.

"Major Snow says that he's requested more tanks and they are on the way from Dak To. He said they're conducting a Thunder Run. What's that?"

"It's a night road march where they fire machine guns and main tank guns on each side of the road while they move. With any luck, that stops potential ambushes. Hope Charlie hasn't planted any mines since the last mine sweep. There's no time for them to do a mine sweep first. They should be here shortly if they don't run into trouble on the way."

Suddenly, we heard heavy automatic weapons from outside the bunker. The Main Hill was under ground attack. I removed my pistol from its holster, hanging on the nail on the wall, and stuck it in my waistband. I glanced to my right at the rear bunker entrance. Sergeant Smith saw me look at the entrance and checked the magazine on his M16. It was loaded. He pulled the charging handle to the rear and released it, sending a round into the chamber. He checked the safety and leaned the weapon against the wall next to him.

A spot report came in stating that an enemy tank had been seen near the water tank at the end of the airstrip. A mixture of AK-47, B-40, 122mm rockets, white phosphorous, mortar rounds, and recoilless rockets pounded the hill, the intensity increasing. I reported the enemy tanks and called for more artillery all around the three hills of the camp as the Special Forces team coordinated the firing of final protective fires. It sounded like the Mad Minute I had experienced before, except this was one hundred times more intense and many of the rounds were headed towards us. AK-47 green tracers mixed with the red tracers of our M16s. Flares lit up the night and Spooky rapidly spit thousands of fiery red tracers around the camp.

The SF team on the West Hill reported three tracked vehicles 800 meters west on route 512 when two explosions highlighted them. Several actions occurred almost simultaneously. Overhead flares illuminated the vehicles when the lead enemy tank fired. At once, our tanks responded with their main guns. Our artillery, mortars, and Spooky all joined in. One of the enemy tanks exploded, its damaged hulk silhouetted by Spooky's flares. Score a hit for our tanks. Round after round of mortar fire and supporting friendly artillery pounded the enemy tank and the nearby road. The flares again revealed the second enemy tank behind the first with another vehicle that looked like an ammunition carrier following. Both tanks were destroyed. The tracked ammo carrier was also destroyed. The lead tank was unrecognizable due to the damage.

"West Hill reports dinks in the wire!" Enemy soldiers had broken into the inner defensive perimeter barbed wire.

Major Snow appeared at my elbow. Pointing at my map, he said, "Give me arty here and here and give me lots of it!"

I called into my handset, "Fire Mission! Fire Mission! Enemy in the wire. I say again, enemy in the wire! Over."

"Roger. Understand. Send targets. Over"

I passed the target numbers with clear urgency in my voice. "Hold on. Rounds will be in the air in a few seconds" came the reply.

He was right. In less than thirty seconds, he said, "Shot out. Rounds on the way. Over."

Seconds later Major Snow yelled out, "Too damned close. Those rounds are too close to our friendlies. They're taking shrapnel. Tell arty to add one hundred meters before we get friendlies killed."

Before I could relay that information, Major Snow said, "Scratch that. It's right on target where it is. Friendlies are hunkered down."

After a few minutes, Major Snow said, "Tell arty 'end of mission' and 'thanks.' Oh yeah, stand by for more targets."

I relayed the info to the fire direction center and asked Major Snow what happened.

He said, "Double check those coordinates. The rounds were close, but they caught Charlie right in the wire. Must have been sappers trying to get inside. Stopped them cold. Got to check on those damned tanks from Dak To. Where are they?" He walked over and picked up the SF radio handset.

I could hear the continuing barrage of rounds impacting above us. I began to speak into the handset of my radio when the air suddenly became caustic. Charlie hit us with another surprise. My eyes immediately teared up, my nose began running, and I felt as though a hand were gripping my throat and crushing my windpipe. My face was burning, but not nearly as bad as my throat. Choking, I reached for my mask and gasped into the handset. "Gas ... gas!"

The anxious voice on the other end of the radio yelled back, "Put your mask on *now!*"

I couldn't respond. Neither could Sergeant Smith. We both were struggling to get our masks on while wiping off the tears and mucus from our faces. I dropped the handset and fought to put my mask on. Finally I had it over my face and could breathe better. I recognized the symptoms of tear gas immediately. Thankfully, it was not something more deadly. I cleared my mask and literally breathed a sigh of relief that it was working properly. Even so, I was nearly incapacitated for a few minutes. Recovering, I bent over and picked up the radio handset off the floor. Incoming rounds still impacted ferociously above me outside the command post.

My speech was slurred and muffled from the mask, but I managed to send my call sign. "This is Lima Six-Three. Over."

Silence. I tried again with no results. My radio appeared to be working. I called again, "Any station this net. This is Lima Six-Three. Over." No response.

I continued trying to reach anyone on the radio net for the next ten minutes without success. Sergeant Smith cautiously removed his mask and called, "All clear. It's safe to remove your masks." I slowly removed mine and wiped my face and neck with my neckerchief. Listening to the explosions from above, I cautiously climbed the short stairs to the bunker entrance. I breathed the night air deeply, feeling instant relief. The night flashed with the explosions as flames and smoke from the nearby ammo bunker lit up the area to my left. Furious machinegun fire sounded from the West Hill in tandem with the barrel flashes.

Pushing past me, Sergeant Smith said, "Sir, I'm going to check the antenna. That may be our problem." He rushed up the stairs and into the night. I stood at the top of the stairs and watched as he checked the antenna. A few minutes later, he returned and said, "Yep. One of the incoming rounds must have cut the guide wires supporting the antenna. It's back in operation. Let's check communications now."

We went back inside the bunker and I tried the radio handset again. "This is Lima Six-Three. Any station this net. Over."

I was rewarded by a response from the tactical CP at Dak To. "We have you loud and clear, Six-Three. We're glad you're back on the net. Thought we lost you for good. Is everything OK? Over."

"Roger. Glad to be back. We're OK for now. We did have a few anxious moments. Still taking incoming but no more gas. Over."

"Any damage? Over."

"The supply and arms room and the ammo bunker all took direct hits. They're still burning. Tracked vehicle noises are being reported near the airstrip. No more reports of casualties yet. Over."

"Roger. The Bravo element is en route and should close your location anytime. Over."

I gave a quick update on the situation and handed the radio handset to Sergeant Smith. "Here. Your turn for a while. I'm going to check on those tanks from Dak To."

As I departed, Sergeant Smith said, "Roger. Curious how all they *all* took direct hits, isn't it? Makes you wonder whether they were blown up from *inside* the camp."

"I've been wondering the same thing. We know that Charlie has infiltrated the camp. It would be easy to throw a satchel charge or two into the ammo or supply bunkers."

I walked over to the front entrance of the command bunker. Major Snow and Captain French were shouting over the noise.

"I can hear our tanks on Route 512. Sounds like they're a click or so away and moving fast," said French.

"Yep. So far, so good. No ambushes or mines. Maybe they caught Charlie off guard along the road. All the attention is focused on us. Charlie thinks it's too dangerous for anything to move on the road at night especially with all the incoming rounds hitting us here."

"Guess so. We sure can use those tanks. If necessary we can use them in direct fire along with the artillery tubes. Those flechette rounds will do a damn-damn on Charlie."

As we watched, the three tanks followed by an ammunition carrier and another tracked vehicle came into view, bearing down on the gate to Main Hill, where we were located. The lead tank didn't slow but crashed through the gate and wheeled around to the left in a 180-degree maneuver that left it facing the direction from which it came. It covered the trailing vehicles as they sped through the gate and rolled on for another thirty meters. The other two tanks faced toward the outside of the defensive perimeter.

"Shock effect. Pretty impressive!"

"Yeah. Go tell the platoon leader to move his tanks to the West Hill," said Major Snow to Captain French as he hustled off to inspect the damaged gate.

For the next several hours, the incoming rounds on our location slowly decreased, and we began receiving reports from our air observers that the enemy was moving their tanks and other vehicles back across the border into Laos and Cambodia. Spooky and friendly artillery chased them along the route, inflicting damage and casualties to the retreating forces.

As the night turned to gray and light began to show on the horizon, it was time to survey the damage and assess needed repairs to the bunkers, vehicles, and other equipment. Ground fog would make visibility difficult until it cleared around 0930. Even so, the damage to the camp was apparent. Enemy casualties included eleven charred bodies in the wire on the West Hill and seven in the perimeter wire on the Main Hill. Pieces of enemy bodies lay scattered around the area. It was apparent from the drag marks and blood trails leading away from the camp that the enemy had evacuated many more dead and wounded in their retreat. The burning ammunition bunker and supply room were still smoldering as the Green Berets carefully looked among the ashes at the tangled and burned gear. Along with a deuce-and-a half, a water trailer, and a three-quarter-ton truck, the destroyed equipment list included flame throwers, recoilless rifles, two .50-caliber machineguns, mortars, grenade launchers, Browning Automatic Weapons (BARs), and one hundred ninety-one .30 caliber carbines. Additionally, 1800 pairs of jungle boots, stacks of blankets and ponchos, and hundreds of uniform items had burned up. Charlie had destroyed virtually all the supplies in the camp with perfectly placed rounds, aided by sabotage.

"Let's get a patrol out there ASAP to check out those destroyed enemy tanks," ordered Captain French. "Be careful. There are still enemy troops in the area and I don't want any more casualties."

When the patrol reached the destroyed tanks, they reported no enemy bodies, but they saw two tanker helmets and burned uniforms scattered around the vehicles. Documents were laying about the wreckage. They recovered Russian technical operating manuals, along with enemy personal diaries, letters, a Chinese poem book, a diploma from the NVA Armor School, and one ID tag. The patrol also reported that the tanks had run over two antitank mines, which had apparently disabled them before our tanks and artillery pounded them. SF personnel had emplaced eight mines in this location the previous September in order to stop any armored vehicle threat. The mines had done their duty well by immobilizing the tanks; however, the enemy tanks were still dangerous because of their main guns. Quick reaction and massive firepower had silenced them. I later found out that this was the only US and enemy tank-on-tank battle of the Vietnam War.

I reported the situation to my headquarters and summarized the casualty count, both enemy and friendly. I also provided a partial list of the major items destroyed in the ammo bunker and elsewhere on the camp. Over four hundred enemy incoming mortar and artillery rounds had pummeled the camp in the first three days of March. Ben Het had taken a beating, but it still stood securely, for now. The enemy had been denied the victory they had greatly wanted so that they could announce to the world how, once again, the invaders had been vanquished.

27
DOWNED PILOT

March 1969

THE F-100 BANKED sharply to the right as the tracers from the enemy antiaircraft machine gun followed it. Light smoke trailed from behind the jet as the persistent tracer rounds kept on target. As we watched, the cockpit flew away and a figure emerged immediately, separating from the injured aircraft. After a few seconds, we saw the parachute canopy opening and I heard myself saying quietly, "All right! The pilot made it."

Standing next to me was Major Snow and the Vietnamese SF Camp Commander, Đi Úy Hue. Captain Hue's wife—or concubine, as I was later told; Hue had several "wives" that periodically visited the camp—was absolutely beautiful, dressed in her gold Vietnamese traditional Áo dài. She obviously had some European ancestry, accenting her lovely features. Although she maintained her distant and refined manner, she appeared to enjoy the sideway glances from her silent admirers.

A few minutes earlier we had been enjoying the show as the Super Sabres unloaded their payload of bombs on the enemy antiaircraft positions. Almost as quickly as the positions were destroyed—within one or two days—they were rebuilt and again spewing rounds at our air observers and FACs. These same positions had been pounded into empty craters by our massive firepower a few days earlier during the ground attack on Ben Het. The NVA had moved their antiaircraft weapons into the prepared positions in advance of their tanks and ground troops in order to provide cover for their movements into final attack positions. They were quickly destroyed by our artillery and aircraft, only to be rebuilt once again in a seemingly never-ending display of determination. Replacement manpower and equipment continued to trickle into the area from the vast encampments across the borders. The massive stockpiling of supplies and personnel in Laos and Cambodia kept this stream of materiel flowing.

During our Super Sabres' impressive show of precision bombing, I thought I saw two enemy tanks in the wood line two thousand meters away. Captain Hue was scanning the air and the distant forest, alternately watching the fighter-bombers and looking for enemy activity on the ground. We knew that the enemy had brought tanks and reconnaissance vehicles back into Vietnam following the siege last week; the FACs had observed the tracks on the trails leading to Route 512. Some of the vehicles had ventured onto the road for a few hundred meters and then moved off into the canopy-covered trails, which provided concealment from the air. Although we had not seen any vehicles, the tracks and engine noises at night told us the NVA was still delivering supplies and personnel as well as performing limited reconnaissance of our defensive perimeters.

"Trung Úy. Where you see tanks?" asked an excited Hue.

I pointed out two dark shadows side by side in the distant tree line. Hue quickly looked through his binoculars in the direction I was pointing and said "Where? Where? I no see!" I heard the fright in his voice.

Looking again, I could no longer see the shadows. If Hue couldn't see them using his binoculars, I concluded that I was wrong. "Đi Úy Hue, I don't see them anymore. It could have just been shadows in the trees if you can't see them."

Hue lowered his binoculars and gave me an annoyed look. He clearly didn't like being embarrassed, even slightly, in front of his wife.

Major Snow looked at me and I thought I detected a small smile on his face for an instant. I suspected there was a bit of animosity between the American and Vietnamese Special Forces, although nothing was said.

The pilot's parachute had opened completely and he drifted in the general direction of the camp. Major Snow turned to Captain French, who had joined us outside the bunker. "Let's get a patrol headed in the direction of that pilot. He may need some help if Charlie locates him first."

"WILCO. We have one in the area. I'll send them toward his location right away," said French.

Just then, the damaged F-100 exploded. We saw parts of the aircraft falling in the jungle to our southwest, and some large fragments were flying in our direction. We quickly ducked into the bunker, staying there a few minutes. Then we moved back outside.

We continued to watch, hoping no enemy fire tried to shoot down the helpless pilot. He continued to drift to our northeast. Good. That was the most secure area between Ben Het and Dak To. There was a much better chance of getting to him before the enemy did. At Fort Benning I had participated in training several times on how to extract a downed pilot and knew that the most dangerous part was establishing contact on the ground without friendly forces shooting at each other. Today that would be especially dangerous, since an excited, and perhaps injured, pilot could easily mistake the CIDG patrol for NVA soldiers. I went back inside the bunker to listen to the radio as the patrol searched for the pilot. Also, I needed to ensure that my headquarters was informed of the rescue efforts.

"Sir, I heard that our tank unit has vehicles standing by in case they're needed to support the pilot rescue," reported Sergeant Smith as I entered the TOC. My eyes slowly adjusted to the dimness inside.

"Good. The patrol is moving in his direction now."

Soon we received the radio call that the pilot had been located and was in friendly hands. He was en route to our location for eventual pickup by the Air Force. I walked outside the TOC when I heard the pilot was coming in.

My first impression of the Air Force lieutenant colonel was that he would be a good target in the jungle. He was over six feet tall, perhaps six-four. His flight suit, fiery red hair, and unusual size were immediate giveaways that he wasn't Oriental or Montagnard. Another, smaller man might have gone unnoticed for a short while among the Vietnamese, but not this fellow. He stood out even among the Americans in the camp

"Colonel, glad to have you with us," said Major Snow as the pilot walked up to our location.

"I can tell you I'm certainly glad to be here instead of out there," he said as he jerked his thumb over his should towards the jungle. "First time I've parachuted. Not as bad as I thought it would be. Thanks to your folks for finding me quickly."

"Yeah. I'm glad, too. The NVA have been pretty unfriendly around here lately. Where did the patrol find you?"

"Well, when I hit the ground I hid my chute and headed toward Route 512. I figured I could make it to your camp and get help from there. I hid in a culvert under the road for a little while until this villager came along on a Moped. I took a chance and hitched a ride with him for a short ways. He let me off, and your folks picked me up shortly afterwards."

"You're lucky the villager was friendly and not VC. Luckily you landed to our east. That gave you a better chance of finding help."

"Yeah. Guess I've just been lucky today. Except, of course, I lost a damn good airplane. Those antiaircraft gunners are pretty good. They got me with .51-caliber machine guns."

"Yeah. We saw your plane explode. Pieces landed nearby. Let's go get a cold one. Might as well get comfortable. Can't get you out until tomorrow."

"Sounds good. Thanks."

I watched them walk away and thought what a lucky fellow this pilot was. He could have been lost in the explosion of his aircraft, shot while parachuting, or killed in the jungle by the NVA who were certainly searching for him. Maybe even worse yet, he could have been captured and made a guest in the Hanoi Hilton, perhaps never to be heard from again. I had heard of stories of captured Americans being tortured in inconceivable manners upon capture while in prison camps. He must have had similar thoughts.

Special Forces Camp A-244, Ben Het. This is an aerial view looking west. Located just eight miles from the tri-border area of Laos-Cambodia-Vietnam, it was manned by US and Vietnamese Special Forces and approximately 400 Civilian Irregular Defense Group (CIDG) mercenaries. (Official US Army photograph)

Destroyed Russian PT-76 tank near Ben Het Special Forces Camp. Two tanks and an armored ammunition carrier were destroyed in March 1969 by US M48A3 tanks of B Company, 1-69th Armor, and a combination of artillery, mortars, gunships, Spooky, and anything else that could be mustered. They were initially disabled by antitank mines, planted the previous September by the US Army Special Forces soldiers.

Another view of the same tank. A result of the only US-
versus-NVA armored tank battle in the Vietnam War.
(Official US Army photograph)

Destroyed PT-76 tank near Ben Het, March 1969. (Official
US Army photograph)

PT-76 tank being prepared for extraction by M88 by
combat engineers from the 299th Engineer Battalion.
(Photograph courtesy of Jay L. Gearhart)

28
ESCAPE PLANS

March 1969

W E'VE GOT A situation here," said Major Snow. "Men, you know that we have two companies of Strike Force units in the camp at this moment: one from Mang Buk and one from Dak Pek. Their mission was to reinforce us. That mission is complete."

Five minutes earlier, all US personnel in the CP were told to assemble in the briefing room. I looked around and counted eight. The other US troops were scattered on the West Hill and with the artillery or tanks. Major Snow appeared somber as he looked around at the assembled group. We were all exhausted from lack of sleep and the stress of constant enemy pressure these past weeks. Even so, Major Snow appeared more haggard than usual. I noticed that most of the Special Forces personnel had weapons with them. My pistol was hanging on the wall in the next room. Usually we did not carry our weapons in the TOC, but kept them close in the event we needed them. Sergeant Smith was manning the radio while I sat in the conference. Behind Snow was the large situation map used to track daily activities, post enemy sightings, and brief VIPs.

Snow cleared his throat and continued, "Both strike units claim they haven't been paid in weeks. They've demanded to be paid immediately and want transportation back to their home locations within twenty-four hours, or they have threatened to kill all US personnel in the camp." He paused to let everyone think about that for a moment. "They've got machine guns at each of the bunker entrances, and their commanders told me that they'll fire on any US personnel attempting to exit. So, first of all, don't leave the TOC. We're talking with them and have alerted the group headquarters of the situation. They expect to get the transportation and money shortly. However, keep your weapons close and be prepared to move quickly, on order."

Moments ago, everyone was still exhilarated at winning the battle with the NVA. Although we knew the enemy had recon elements all around us, we were not expecting any major activity during the lull that followed the siege. Neither were we expecting our former allies to turn their guns on us. Tension gave way to anger, and several personnel stated that we should just bust out of the TOC and attack the mutinous strike units. We might have done just that, but we were outnumbered by at least twenty to one and they had the advantage of emplaced machine guns. We were also isolated, and to break out we would be channeled directly into their sights.

As difficult as the situation was, it could get worse, and the only alternative might be to assault the machine guns. That would be a very bloody affair and likely only a few of us would escape. There was a very good chance that none would survive. The tanks and artillery were in a similar predicament and wouldn't be able to offer much support in a firefight with the strike units.

"Here's the plan if things get worse," said Major Snow. "We have to be prepared to escape." He described the plan: A small group would attempt to exit the front entrance and create a diversion while the main group of six or seven burst out the rear entrance and overwhelmed the machine gun there. Once outside the bunker, it would be every man for himself. Survivors should attempt to pair up with each other and travel in two-man groups. Prior to that, the camp escape plan called for the codebooks and any sensitive equipment to be destroyed, except for the radios, which would be taken in order to contact the anticipated rescue element. That element would have to come from Dak To and would take at least an hour, barring delays. Survivors were to follow Route 512 east to Dak To, staying in the jungle to avoid detection. We did not know whether Charlie had ambushes and patrols along the route. We would have to assume they did and avoid them, if possible.

"I'm not going to kid you. It will be extremely risky, but, if we have to evacuate, it's our only chance of success. I want everyone to check their weapons and ammunition. Stand by until you hear from me."

Sergeant Smith had heard part of the discussion and was standing near the door as I left the meeting. "Damn. This might get real hairy!"

"It just might. Let's check our maps and see what we will have to destroy in case we have to execute the escape plan." I couldn't help thinking that it wasn't much of an escape plan, but I couldn't come up with one any better.

Another hour passed in the tension-filled bunker while we awaited word on the transportation and money from the Special Forces headquarters. I thought of every possible contingency in the event we would have to break out. I envisioned throwing grenades out both entrances first, then rushing out of the door behind the explosions. Engaging the machine guns was the first order of business, since any chance of survival relied on stopping that concentrated firing. Secondly, we would have to take out any support positions, since it was highly likely there were other automatic weapons directed at the entrances. Should we have to break out, I didn't give us much of a chance of survival. Perhaps if we could get supporting fire from Cobra gunships on those gun positions before we ran up the stairs ...

I looked up from my map at Major Snow as he walked over to me. "We can relax. Transportation is on the way for the strike units and we have received a helicopter full of piasters to pay them. Looks like the immediate danger is over."

"Thanks, sir. I was not anxious to break out of here."

"Me neither. Our chances weren't very good. Anyway, it's over. By the way, after chow tonight we're going to hold a little party to welcome the new camp commander, Captain Queenly. It'll be in the team house. I figure we all deserve some relaxation." Snow left smiling.

Sergeant Smith unloaded his weapon, put it aside, and said, "I heard the SF medic went on a mission to pick up some special cargo a few minutes ago. He left in a jeep pulling a trailer headed towards Dak To."

"Interesting. Wonder what he went to pick up."

Later that evening after all reports were sent and I had finished my C-ration dinner, I climbed the dirt stairs and went outside. It was getting dark, and at the moment there were no incoming rounds. Charlie had left us alone for the past several hours. Perhaps we could relax for a while.

Inside the damaged team house, other than the few remaining personnel on radio watch, the SF team were relaxing and enjoying the cold Tiger Beer. "Grab a beer, LT," said one of the SF sergeants. "The entertainment starts shortly."

I promised myself to have just one. I said, "Thanks. Entertainment?"

The sergeant grinned and went back to his beer.

After a short while, the special cargo was brought in. To my surprise, it consisted of three "business" girls from a village near Dak To. The ladies of the evening arrived riding in the trailer hitched to the back of the medic's jeep. A layer of hastily wiped dust still covered their faces like pancake makeup. These ladies were shopworn and about as enticing as another enemy mortar round. Whore ran to greet them, barking as she loped up to the trailer. There seemed to be an instant rapport between them.

To collect the "entertainment," the medic had taken a rough and dangerous ride over a road frequently mined and ambushed by Charlie. Route 512 was the same dirt road that the speeding friendly M-48 tanks had traveled a few nights before to reinforce the camp during the ground attack. Others might call that second ride reckless, but the SF team preferred to think of it as daring. The remainder of the raucous evening consisted of beer drinking and celebration. It was also an initiation for the new camp commander. It was the kind of merriment that men who have survived danger together can enjoy together. Not all participated in the favors offered by the business girls, but a few did. The evening was getting too racy for me, so I excused myself and headed to my bunk for a few hours of what I hoped would be uninterrupted sleep.

Several days later, I was ordered back to the brigade base camp. Mixed emotions flooded my thoughts. I had survived a tough battle alongside this SF team, and although I was still an outsider, I sensed there was mutual respect between us. Part of me felt I was abandoning them, although I knew that was foolish, since these men were proven combat veterans who knew what it took to survive. I watched Ben Het disappear over my shoulder from the chopper and wished them luck. I was returning to my mundane duties for my last few months until rotation back to the world.

29
MEDEVAC

April 1969

A COUSTIC AND SEISMIC sensors were concealed from view in the tent, according to Parkins. "That's what they are. They're made to look like small trees, and we drop them along the Ho Chi Minh Trail and other spots where the VC or NVA have been moving recently."

On my way to breakfast, I noticed that the normally open windows on the newly erected tent alongside the mess tent were closed. Wondering what was inside, I lifted the canvas flap and saw two rows of green plants three feet high. They were laid out neatly and each had a tag affixed. The bottom of each tree protruded from a pointed canister, also painted green. I thought, *This has got to be some kind of new bomb.*

Jerry Parkins put his coffee cup on the table and sat next to me on the bench. I had finished breakfast and was preparing to report to the TOC. Since Jerry was assigned to the S2 or intelligence office, I thought he might know what the strange plant-like items were. I asked him.

"We're going to deploy them later today in the Plei Trap Valley. When the VC or NVA pass nearby, the sensors send a signal alerting us and we can call in preplanned artillery on that location. Or we can just monitor the movement for a few days to get an idea of how often the VC use those roads for infiltration into our area of operations."

"That's pretty cool," I said. "Have we been using these very long?"

"Not here. They've been using them farther north along the Ho Chi Minh Trail. There're a couple of different variants that pick up vehicle noises and vibrations. By the way, keep this to yourself. It's a classified program. Not for general knowledge."

"Can do."

The door to the mess tent opened quickly, then slammed shut behind Specialist Fifth Class Keaton. "Lieutenant Evans! Captain Trotter wants to see you right away." Spec 5 Keaton was one of the radio operators in the TOC.

I reached for my helmet and stood up. "See you later. Time to work."

I hurried to the TOC and saw Captain Trotter standing at the entrance.

"Frank, go to the helicopter pad. There's a slick on the way in to pick you up. There's been an accident at the Kontum Bridge and an ARVN soldier is badly hurt."

"What happened?" I asked

"From what we have been told, one of his buddies fired a 90mm recoilless rifle at a suspected VC position across the river. He forgot to check the back blast area and the injured soldier was standing immediately behind him. He took the full force of the blast. Understand he's pretty messed up. We need you to accompany him to Pleiku Hospital in the chopper. There's no time to find a medic. You've got to hustle."

"Roger, sir. On the way."

I ran down the hill to the landing pad. Thirty seconds later the chopper landed and I jumped aboard. The door gunner yelled in my ear, "Sir, we're going to pick up a wounded ARVN at the Dak Bla Bridge. He's hurt real bad. Need you to keep him from choking to death while we take him to the hospital."

"Roger," I yelled back.

The slick lifted off and we headed north to the bridge. We landed four minutes later near a stretcher held by two ARVN soldiers. The soldier in the stretcher had blood streaming from his mouth, nose, and ears. At first I wasn't sure he was alive, but he was semi-conscious. Another soldier held his head to the side to keep him from choking on his blood. They quickly loaded the stretcher onto the chopper and I steadied the wounded soldier's head, holding it to the side.

As the soldiers moved away from the chopper, we lifted off, swung around to the south, and gained elevation. I had never been this close to an ARVN soldier. I didn't have much respect for them as soldiers. They were ill trained and poorly motivated, but this fellow was badly wounded and probably wouldn't make it. I felt sorry for him. He was losing a lot of blood and his eyes were out of focus. He had to be in a great amount of pain, too. I realized that he was not only hurting but also terrified. I hoped he stayed alive long enough to get him to the hospital so the doctors could have a chance to save him. All I could do was offer some comfort and keep his mouth clear of blood.

Although it was difficult to look at him because of all the blood, I made sure his head was turned to the side and his mouth was open. His jaw was broken. I inserted three fingers of my right hand into his mouth to keep it open and held his head with my left hand. He looked up at me, and I could read the helplessness in his eyes. A tear crept from the corner of his eye and mixed with blood on his cheek. I nodded and tried a small smile, hoping it would reassure him. He noticed, and I thought I saw a small smile form at the corner of his eyes. He appreciated my efforts, however small they were.

We landed at the Pleiku Hospital and a nurse and two medics came out to get the soldier. The medics picked up the stretcher and carried him to the emergency room. That was the last I saw him. Although I wondered about his fate, I never found out what became of him. From that point on, I never thought of ARVN soldiers as faceless beings. They might not be as professional as we hoped, but each soldier was an individual, and I put a human face on each one after my experience with this dying soldier.

The slick lifted off and returned me to the base camp.

30
VISUAL RECON

May 1969

I SAW THE object just as Warrant Officer First Class
Logan's voice came over my helmet's headset. "Here, catch,"
he said. Instinctively I grabbed the green object out of the air
and made sure the grenade pin was still in place. Tear gas grenade, one each, OD (olive drab) in color.

"Nice throw," I said. "What if I had dropped this inside the
cockpit? We'd both be gulping rice paddy water after we
crashed."

Smiling, Logan said, "I see you have already noticed the pin
is in place. No harm done. I've got two more here."

"And what am I supposed to do with these?"

"We'll drive the villagers away from the dump near the protective wire. G2 thinks they're reconing the wire for an easy

entrance. VC hit the engineer compound near here recently, remember?"

"Yeah. The sappers sneaked in through the protective wire and blew up several bunkers and a couple of personnel carriers. I wrote a report on that, as a matter of fact."

"Well, the G2 doesn't want a repeat, so orders are to keep all indigenous personnel away from the wire. Lieutenant Parkins gave me the CS grenades to use."

Logan and I were flying at three hundred feet two kilometers west of the brigade base camp. We were conducting the early morning VR, or visual reconnaissance, around the camp to look for any suspicious activity, like enemy mortar positions or rockets and such. Twice daily, Captain Barren or I joined one of the LOH pilots in this task. It was a good break from the daily duties and the stuffy air inside the TOC. Usually we observed nothing out of the ordinary. If we did spot something unusual, we would radio back to the TOC for a patrol to check it out.

Earlier in the flight, Logan and I had circled to the south and east of the camp as far north as the Dak Bla River Bridge on the outskirts of Kontum. Kontum was a good-sized town that had flowered into a beautiful small city during the French colonial period. Now it had been mortared and rocketed into a war-torn eyesore, with only remnants of its former beauty. Strands of concertina wire, bunkers, guard posts, and ARVN soldiers, riding in military vehicles or listlessly walking the streets, contributed to its dull, dingy appearance. Barefoot Montagnard men and women carried their baskets of roots, fish, and vegetables to the marketplace.

At this time of day, early morning, the Vietnamese townspeople were beginning to venture out of their dwellings, and occasionally a Vietnamese or Eurasian woman dressed in the traditional *ao dai* could be seen headed to the marketplace or local meat market. Another uneasy night of sporadic firing and distant explosions had passed. The VC had retreated into obscurity and the ARVN soldiers were cautiously patrolling the streets once again. American military deuce-and-a-half trucks were en route to the water point, or fueling site.

Approaching the bridge at a low altitude, Logan winked and said, "Watch this maneuver." Before I could ask, "What maneuver?" we were skimming the top of the river and headed straight towards the bridge. Next to us on the right side were two canoes with loincloth-wearing Montagnard men standing and guiding their vessels with long poles. They looked incredulously at us as we flew by. I imagine they were thinking, *Americans!* Diên cái đu! Crazy! I had to agree.

It was too late for us to gain altitude, so I just said, "You crazy son of a bitch!" He smiled more broadly.

Directly ahead of us under the bridge, I saw a sagging cable hanging low from one bank of the river to the other. It was only fifteen or twenty feet above the water, sagging in the middle. I shouted at Logan over my intercom, "*Look out!* We're going to hit that cable!" Just before we slammed into the cable, Logan maneuvered to the left and we shot under the cable with inches to spare.

"Man, I didn't know that was there," Logan said, still smiling. He saw the look on my face and knew how near he was to getting choked to death. "Relax. I was only kidding. All us pilots do that with a new guy in the cockpit. Now tell me that wasn't great!"

I didn't respond for a few moments. "First of all, I'm not a new guy. I'm getting close to the end of my tour. And second, don't take unnecessary chances. There's enough real danger out there to kill us. We don't need to invent more." I was fuming at the joke he had played on me. There wasn't time to be scared, but there was plenty of time to be angry afterwards. We followed the river for several hundred meters before Logan said, "OK. Let me show you something else."

"No more swooping under bridges for me. I've had enough. I made it this far and I don't plan to get killed doing something stupid. Thank you."

"OK, LT. This is tame. See those large mats spread out along the riverbank near the deuce-and-a-halves?"

"Yeah. So?"

"Watch what happens as we fly close."

Logan dropped our altitude once again and slowed our speed. As we neared the riverbank dust began to swirl up and the wind blew against the mats. Suddenly two mats, then another, lifted up and blew away exposing the occupants of the small dugout caves in the side of the riverbank. Three naked Vietnamese females, accompanied by three semi-dressed GIs hunkered over them, gestured and shouted at us angrily. We had rudely intruded into their private moments and no doubt blown grit and sand into their … activities. Logan laughed loudly and gained altitude quickly. I guess this show was his way of making up.

I couldn't help laughing along with him.

We turned south and headed back toward the base camp as I held the tear gas grenade in my hand. We approached the camp and I saw ten or twelve individuals in the middle of the dump-site scavenging for food or scraps of metal or whatever they could find that was useful. There were several young boys and a few old men.

"There's the villagers poking about in the dump. They could be reconing our defenses also," said Logan.

"Unfortunately there's no way to tell, so I guess we have to run them away before they accidentally set off a claymore mine—or some trigger-happy bunker guard decides to fire at them."

"Yes. I'll fly in close and you toss the tear gas grenades near them. That should move them away from the defensive perimeter."

"OK."

Logan positioned the chopper between the fence and the scavengers about fifty feet in the air. We didn't want the trash and smells of the dump coming up around us. I threw one grenade near two young men, who immediately ran in the opposite direction. Logan hovered the chopper thirty meters to the right and I threw another gas grenade. They popped and began filling the area with white smoke. Before we got a whiff of gas, Logan gained altitude and moved away two hundred meters upwind.

"Uh, oh. Look at the smoke!"

"Oh, shit!" I yelled. "We are going to be in big trouble now."

"What you mean 'we,' Lone Ranger?" joked Logan. "You threw the grenades. Plus, you are the ranking officer on this mission."

"Thanks. So that's the way it is."

I watched as the smoke began to drift rapidly into our brigade base camp, over the bunkers, and directly toward the brigade command post. The bunker guards were getting a heavy dose of the gas now. Everyone inside the TOC would soon get a good dose, and if I guessed correctly, the brigade commander would have already finished breakfast and be inside receiving his early morning briefings with his staff.

While I watched, Lieutenant Parkins came running out of our tent next to the TOC. He was shaking his head and trying to cover his eyes with his arms as he struggled with his mask. He glanced up toward our chopper and raised a fist in the air. Actually, it would have been a fist, except for the one finger extended straight up. He was very angry and very uncomfortable. It would have been hilarious if I didn't know the kind of hell I was going to get upon my return. I got along well with the senior staff officers and the brigade CO, but I wasn't sure that would be the case after they got a strong dose of tear gas. I remembered my recent experience with it.

Sitting erect in my seat, clenching my teeth, and putting on my best John Wayne voice, I said, "Well, Mister Logan, shall we go face the firing squad?"

He turned the chopper in the direction of the landing pad. "Guess we don't have any choice, do we, Kemo Sabe?"

31

BACK TO THE WORLD

July 1969

I WAS ON the way back to the world: Columbus, Georgia. My emotions were once again mixed. My wife waited there, and I had plans to make with her. What would we do? Stay in the army? We had discussed it briefly, and I had extended my army tour long enough to make captain, giving us more time to decide on future career plans. I put those thoughts aside and focused on my immediate future. Ahead was Cam Rahn Bay and the beginning of the long flight home.

Home? That was a strange word. My home had been the jungle and dusty camps for the past year. Again, that guilty feeling of abandoning my friends and troops crept up on me. I was torn between the intense desire to see my wife and leave this country and my desire to stay just a little longer here. Here was the first time that I had felt that I was contributing to something larger than my own needs. I'm not sure that it was patriotism I felt, although I guess anyone could label it that. I loved my country and was proud of my contributions. I knew that my family was proud. I had been a leader in this remote place and shared friendships and relationships with other people like none I'd experienced before. People had counted on me to make important decisions, and I felt confident I was making the right ones.

I finally convinced myself that I was glad to be leaving Vietnam. If I had remained or extended my tour in country, I would have spent my time there on the brigade staff. Most of the guys I knew there had already left. I didn't particularly like the base camp environment. I was more at ease with a rifle platoon or with the Special Forces soldiers. Besides, my next tour in Vietnam would probably be as a company commander, and I had that to look forward to if I stayed in the army. I was beginning to think like my old high school friend. Was I destined to be a soldier, too?

The next twenty-four hours in Cam Rahn Bay went quickly. There I received a urine test, haircut, clean khaki uniform, shined boots, and I converted my MPC back to greenbacks. Lieutenant Mike Warden and I headed to the officers' club on our last evening. Early next morning we would be boarding the Freedom Plane on the way stateside. Mike and I had gone through OCS together, arrived in country together, and now we were going home together. It was time to celebrate. A group of us who had arrived in Vietnam at the same time shared drinks and stories. Many of us had not seen each other during the past year. We probably wouldn't see each other again, unless we met on another assignment. Many were leaving the army, so it was doubtful we would cross paths. The celebration had that kind of feeling: here's to all, good luck, and good-bye!

Sleep escaped me that last night. I lay awake thinking of the past and the future, all mixed together. Suddenly an explosion jarred me fully awake. Then two, three explosions followed by automatic weapon's fire breaking the night's stillness. I reached for my pistol, which I kept next to my head on the floor. Damn! No weapon. I had turned that in when I left the brigade the day before yesterday. I slipped my boots on as someone yelled to head for the makeshift bunker outside. I looked at my watch. It was almost dawn. Stand to!

I ran outside following the other officers and crawled into the concrete bunker covered with plastic sandbags filled with dirt. At each end of the culvert was a sandbag wall protecting each entrance from shell fragments. We were packed inside as we listened to the continuing explosions and weapons. I could see the flashes of the explosions and saw that a couple were no more than a hundred yards away. I felt helpless and claustrophobic. Voices outside the bunker must have been from soldiers responding to the attack.

"Where we going, Sergeant?"

"Heading toward the hospital. That's where they saw the sappers," yelled another soldier. "Watch where you shoot. Don't want to hit any patients."

I thought, *Dammit. I have made it through a hell of a year and now I'm going to get wounded or killed on my last night here.* I wasn't particularly scared, but I was as mad as hell. The time for us to board our flight home came and went. All incoming aircraft had to be turned away due to the attack on Cam Rahn Bay.

Finally, the firing and explosions ended. An hour later, we were informed that the sapper attack was over and we could come outside the bunker. I was sore, tired, and still mad. After a short breakfast, we were directed to a bus and taken to the flight line to board another Freedom Bird. At last I was on my way home. Months later, I found out that my platoon sergeant, Sergeant Mayer, was in the Cam Rahn Bay hospital recovering from malaria at the time of the sapper attack. He suffered a broken leg when a satchel charge thrown by an enemy sapper exploded and tossed a five-gallon water can down the aisle between the beds, hitting him in the leg. Fortunately, he recovered from both the illness and the injury.

The flight home was long, but I slept through most of it. I think there was a movie, but I didn't care. We landed in San Francisco, where we were met by a sergeant who briefed us on the airport and told us to ignore the radicals. "If they curse you, ignore it. They're only a small group, and we're trying to keep them away from returning flights. Welcome home, guys."

My first stop was a bar. I didn't encounter any peaceniks there, but I spotted some farther down the corridor but they were headed in the other direction. I downed my drink and caught my flight to Atlanta. Changing flights there, I was less than an hour from Columbus. I had been celebrating all the way from the West Coast, and the rum and Cokes almost made me miss my connecting flight. With the help of a friendly gate person, I managed to get on the correct flight without any trouble. I was getting very anxious now to see my wife again. The plane landed and I started to get up. Fortunately, the seatbelt pulled me back into my seat and we rolled to a stop.

I stood and surveyed the crowd waiting outside for my wife. It was difficult to pick her out of that mass of waiting family and friends, so I climbed down the stairs searching from side to side. Not seeing her, I turned toward the terminal and thought, *She must be inside.* For the second time in my life, I heard the penetrating voice behind me, "Frank ... *Frannnk!* Didn't you see me? I've been chasing you," she said.

Oh, boy. Not again!

32
STAND DOWN

February 1993

M Y TIME AS a soldier had come to a close. It was time to
"stand down" and rely on others to continue serving. Just
like the many stand downs that I had participated in, it was
again time to take a deep breath, relax, and let the sentries take
over. Like untold soldiers before me, my career had taken me to
countless wonderful, exciting, dirty, insect-and snake-infested,
and downright dangerous places. I had visited or served in
numerous stateside military installations from Georgia to
Hawaii to Arizona to New Jersey, which I recollected vividly.
Journeys to exotic places like Panama, Guam, Saipan, Tinian,
American Samoa, Australia, Japan, and Korea developed in me
a respect for the beliefs and traditions of far-flung cultures. Of
the few treasures I planned to bequeath to my children, respect
for others was a gift I hoped they willingly accepted.

I listened to the kind words of the general as he spoke upon my retirement of my twenty-six-year career in the army, and I thought of my friends and acquaintances who shared my journeys. I thought of my friend, Glenn. I wished he could be here to share in this special time. His dream had always been to be a soldier and he had done so for a short time. If you believed in reincarnation, as he had, you might suppose that even now he was serving somewhere in uniform in another life as the soldier he was forever destined to be.

My family and I walked to the elevator as we departed the general's office. Around us were all the friends and soldiers I had served alongside throughout my career in those faraway places. To my right, at rigid attention, stood the toughest little banty rooster basic training drill sergeant, Staff Sergeant Wolfe. I could almost hear him say, "Drop and give me twenty pushups, shitbird!" Next to him was a squad of platoon sergeants, first sergeants, and sergeants major also standing at attention, carefully checking out my military dress and deportment. They had been my teachers and critics throughout the years, and I sought advice and counsel from them. Flanking them I saw the faces of men I hadn't seen in many years: buddies from OCS, young lieutenants I had served with, and even my old roommate and ranger buddy. I glanced to my left and saw another squad of soldiers. There was the platoon sergeant who taught me to be a combat leader. Both of my company commanders from Vietnam were there, exactly as I remembered them.

Lining the long hallway to the elevator were familiar soldiers in various uniforms. Although not physically present, these men were there just the same in my thoughts. They would be there for the rest of my life. I straightened my shoulders and blinked back the mist clouding my eyes. I looked down at my children and thought, *I hope you have memories like these that you can cherish one day.*

33
EPILOGUE

Present Day

C OMBAT IS A unique and highly personal experience. For those of us who survived, it remains an important part of our memories. Thoughts often turn to those we remember who didn't survive, those who sacrificed their futures. They have forever influenced the survivors in some way and helped shape the individuals we have become.

My military career was exciting and extremely satisfying. Not only did I meet numerous influential personalities, but I have worked alongside some of the most dedicated and selfless people that I have ever met. They give much and expect little. They are family oriented and mission focused.

The Vietnam experience was a focal point in the lives of my contemporaries, my family, and my friends. It was a turbulent period for us. Today we are living in another tumultuous and dangerous period. The television news coverage brings back memories of that earlier time. In contrast to the television coverage of the past, today's coverage isn't confined to the evening news. It is available twenty-four hours a day and is instantaneous and more graphic than it was thirty years ago. I am not sure which delivery I prefer more. Sometimes I think I would like to confine the daily news to a short half hour before dinner and leave the remaining hours to more enjoyable activities. I can't do that. World events influence all of us. We can't allow ourselves to ignore the good and bad things that go on around us. That realization was the beginning of my journey to manhood that began those forty or so years ago.

Ho Chi Minh Trail marker on present-day Ben Het site. Only
small reminders of the camp remain, a boot sole here or a
ripped sandbag there.
(Photograph courtesy of Jackson H. Day)

Villagers travel through the former Ben Het SF camp on the
remaining dirt roads that cross the site. They seem oblivious
of the battles that occurred there. (Photograph courtesy of
Jackson H. Day)

34

BEN HET AT DUSK

by Jackson H. Day

It is still, now.

A breeze brings coolness as we stand
where soldiers once built sanctuaries of sandbags.
Clouds shadow the place where steel flew
and imagination tormented.

We look down at the expanse of green hiding old memories,
Covering the tortured earth, all except the airstrip's skeleton.
The red clay of the airstrip's ruins, long bare of its metal surface
glows brighter as the light fades.

Across the road and beyond the stream, mountains rise,
their tops hidden by clouds.

Those who walked among them are now memories,
ghosts who wait to be invoked,
recalled to life by us who once knew them.

They are gone now, all of them,
both to death and to life;
those in bunkers who faced the mountain,
and their enemies moving quietly through the forest.
Gone the fear, gone the misery, gone the pain.

In their place, settlers have built houses by the road.
Peace has come, and peace's possibilities.
As night falls, families share food in lighted rooms.

In nearby towns red posters celebrate victories and heroes.
The young hope they too may one day know such glory.

>   Jackson H. Day
>   Former Chaplain, Fourth Infantry Division
>   Ben Het, Vietnam
>   June 4, 2000
>   Used by permission of Jackson H. Day.

Local Montagnards walking west through the former Ben
Het site. The mountains in the distance are in Cambodia.
Once they hid thousands of NVA soldiers and vast amounts
of vehicles and equipment. NVA artillery fired on Ben Het
from concrete reinforced caves in the sides of those
mountains.
(Photograph courtesy of Jackson H. Day)

GLOSSARY

AAR: after-action report.

AK-47: Soviet-manufactured Kalashnikov semi-automatic and fully automatic combat assault rifle, 7.62-mm; the basic weapon of the Communist forces. Known as the Type 56 to the Chinese, it is characterized by an explosive popping sound.

AO: area of operations.

Áo dài: traditional dress of Vietnamese women. A brightly colored silk top worn over loose fitting silk trousers.

APC: armored personnel carrier. A track vehicle used to transport Army troops or supplies, usually armed with a .50-caliber machine gun.

Arc light: code name for B-52 bombers strikes along the Cambodian-Vietnamese border. These operations shook earth for ten miles away from the target area.

Arty: shorthand term for artillery.

Arvin: soldier in the ARVN, or the ARVN itself.

ARVN: Army of the Republic of Vietnam; the South Vietnamese Regular Army.

B-40 rocket: a shoulder-held rocket-propelled grenade launcher.

B-52: U.S. Air Force high-altitude bomber; also, slang for a can opener.

Base camp: a resupply base for field units and a location for headquarters of brigade or division size units, artillery batteries and air fields. Also known as the rear area.

Battery: an artillery unit equivalent to a company. Six 105mm or 155mm howitzers or two 8-inch or 175mm self-propelled howitzers.

BDA: bomb damage assessment.

Bird: any aircraft, but usually refers to helicopters bird dog: forward air controller

Breaking squelch: disrupting the natural static of a radio by depressing the transmit bar on another radio set to the same frequency.

Brigade: a tactical and administrative military unit composed of a headquarters and one or more battalions of infantry or armor, with other supporting units.

Bush: infantry term for the field.

C-4: plastic, putty textured explosive carried by infantry soldiers. Often used to heat C-rations.

C-123: small cargo airplane; the Caribou.

C-130: large propeller-driven Air Force planes that carry people and cargo; the Hercules.

C-141: large cargo airplane; the Starlifter.

CA: combat assault. The term is used to describe landing soldiers into a hot LZ via helicopter.

Carbine: a short-barreled, lightweight automatic or semiautomatic rifle.

Caribou: small transport plane for moving men and material.

Cav: Cavalry; the 1st Cavalry Division (Airmobile).

Charlie: Việt Cộng.

Chicom: Chinese communist.

Chiêu Hồi: the "open arms" program, promising clemency and financial aid to Việt Cộng and NVA soldiers and cadres who stopped fighting and returned to South Vietnamese government authority.

Chinook: CH-47 cargo helicopter.

Chopper: helicopter.

CIB: combat infantry badge. An Army award for being under enemy fire in a combat zone, worn on both fatigues and dress uniforms.

CIDG: civilian irregular defense groups.

Civilian Irregular Defense Group: American financed, irregular military units led by members of Special Forces A-teams. Members of these units were Vietnamese nationals, but were usually members of ethnic minorities in the country.

Claymore: an antipersonnel mine when detonated, propelled small steel projectiles in a 60-degree fan shaped pattern to a maximum distance of 100 meters.

CO: commanding officer.

Cobra: an AH-1G attack helicopter. Also known as a gunship, armed with rockets and machine guns.

Commo: shorthand for "communications".

Commo wire: communications wire.

Company: a military unit usually consisting of a headquarters and two or more platoons.

Concertina wire: coiled barbed wire used as an obstacle.

Contact: firing on or being fired upon by the enemy.

CP: command post.

C-rations: combat rations. Canned meals for use in the field. Each usually consisted of a can of some basic course, a can of fruit, a packet of some type of dessert, a packet of powdered cocoa, a small pack of four cigarettes, and two pieces of chewing gum.

CS: a riot-control gas which burns the eyes and mucus membranes.

Deuce-and-a-half: two-and-a-half ton truck.

Dink: derogatory term for VC or NVA soldier.

Dinky dau: to be crazy, from"điên cái đu".

Doc: medic or corpsman.

Dust-off: medical evacuation by helicopter.

Elephant grass: tall, razor-edged tropical plant indigenous to certain parts of Vietnam.

Evac'd: evacuated.

F-4: Phantom jet fighter-bombers. Range: 1,000 miles. Speed: 1400 mph. Payload: 16,000 lbs. The workhorse of the tactical air support fleet.

F-100: The Super Sabre was a jet fighter aircraft that flew extensively over South Vietnam as the Air Force's primary close air support jet.

FAC: forward air controller; a person who coordinates air Strikes.

Fast mover: an F-4 or F-100.

Fatigues: standard combat uniform, green in color.

FB: firebase.

FDC: fire direction control center.

Finger charge: explosive booby-trapping device which takes its name from the size and shape's being approximately that of a man's finger.

Fire base: temporary artillery encampment used for fire support of forward ground operations.

Firefight: a battle, or exchange of small arms fire with the enemy.

Flare: illumination projectile; hand-fired or shot from artillery, mortars, or air.

Flechette: a small dart-shaped projectile clustered in an explosive warhead. A mine without great explosive power containing small pieces of shrapnel intended to wound and kill.

FNG: fucking new guy

FO: forward observer. A person attached to a field unit to coordinate the placement of direct or indirect fire from ground, air, and naval forces.

Foo gas: a mixture of explosives and napalm, usually set in a fifty-gallon drum.

FRAGO: fragmentary order. An abbreviated military order.

Freedom Bird: the plane that took soldiers from Vietnam back to the World.

French fort: a distinctive triangular structure built by the hundreds by the French.

Freq: radio frequency.

Green Berets: U.S. Special Forces.

Grunt: infantryman.

Gunship: armed helicopter.

Hamlet: a small rural village.

Hooch: a hut or simple dwelling, either military or civilian

H&I: harassment and interdiction. Artillery bombardments used to deny the enemy terrain which they might find beneficial to their campaign; general rather than specific, confirmed military targets; random artillery fire.

Hercules: a C-130.

Hồ Chí Minh slippers: sandals made from tires. The soles are made from the tread and the straps from inner tubes.

Hot LZ: a landing zone under enemy fire.

Howitzer: a short cannon used to fire shells at medium velocity and with relatively high trajectories.

HQ: headquarters.

Huey: nickname for the UH-1 series helicopters.

Hump: march or hike carrying a rucksack; to perform any arduous task.

II Corps: the Central Highlands military region in South Vietnam.

Illum: an illumination flare, usually fired by a mortar or artillery weapon.

In-country: Vietnam.

Ka-Bar: combat knife.

KIA: killed in action.

Kit Carson scout: former Việt Cộng who act as guides for U.S. military units.

Klick: kilometer

LOH: pronounced Loach. A light observation helicopter

LP: listening post. A two-or three-man position set up at night outside the perimeter away from the main body of troopers, which acted as an early warning system against attack. Also, an amphibious landing platform used by infantry for storming beaches from the sea.

LRRP: Long Range Reconnaissance Patrol. An elite team usually composed of five to seven men who go deep into the jungle to observe enemy activity without initiating contact.

LT: lieutenant.

LZ: landing zone. Usually a small clearing secured lemporarily for the landing of resupply helicopters. Some become more permanent and eventually become base camps.

M-16: the standard U.S. military rifle used in Vietnam from 1966 on. Successor to the M-14.

M-60: the standard lightweight machine gun used by U.S. forces in Vietnam.

M-79: a U.S. military hand-held grenade launcher.

Mad minute: a procedure where all weapons were fired at once, usually to discourage enemy from sneaking up on a friendly position.

Main Force Battalion: the primary Việt Cộng fighting force within each province of South Vietnam.

Medevac: medical evacuation from the field by helicopter.

MoH: Medal of Honor. The highest U.S. military decoration awarded for conspicuous gallantry at the risk of life above and beyond the call of duty.

Montagnard: a French term for several tribes of mountain people inhabiting the hills and mountains of central and northern

Vietnam. Vietnam was a former French Colony and some of their phrases carried forth from their French Colonial days.

Mortar: a muzzle-loading cannon with a short tube in relation to its caliber that throws projectiles with low muzzle velocity at high angles.

Napalm: a jellied petroleum substance which burns fiercely, and is used as a weapon against personnel.

NCO: noncommissioned officer. Usually a squad leader or platoon sergeant.

NDP: night defensive position.

Net: radio frequency setting, from "network."

No sweat: Slang for easy, simple.

NPD: night perimeter defense.

Nùng: tribespeople of Chinese origin, from the highlands of North Vietnam. Some who moved South worked with the U.S. Special Forces.

NVA: North Vietnamese Army.

OCS: officer candidate school.

P-38: a tiny collapsible can opener, also known as a John Wayne.

Perimeter: outer limits of a military position. The area beyond the perimeter belongs to the enemy.

Point or pointman: the forward man or element on a combat patrol

Pop smoke: to ignite a smoke grenade to signal an aircraft.

POW: prisoner of war.

PRC-25: Portable Radio Communications, Model 25. A back-packed FM receiver-transmitter used for short-distance communications. The range of the radio was 5–10 kilometers, depending on the weather, unless attached to a special, non-portable antenna which could extend the range to 20–30 kilometers.

Puff the Magic Dragon: AC-47 is a propeller-driven aircraft with 3 Miniguns—capable of firing 6,000 rounds per minute per gun for a total of 18,000 rounds per minute—The mini guns were on one side of the plane. The plane would bank to one side to fire.

Punji stakes: sharpened bamboo sticks used in a primitive but effective pit trap. They were often smeared with excrement to cause infection.

Purple Heart: U.S. military decoration awarded to any member of the Armed Forces wounded by enemy action. Any soldier awarded three of them was allowed to leave the Vietnam theater.

PZ: pick up zone.

QUAD-50s: a four-barreled assembly of .50 caliber machine guns

RBF: reconnaissance by fire.

Recon: reconnaissance.

Redleg: Artillery or artilleryman.

REMF: rear-echelon motherfucker.

RPG: rocket-propelled grenade. A Russian-made portable anti-tank grenade launcher.

RTO: radio telephone operator. The man who carried his leader's radio on his back in the field. Responsible for maintaining communications.

Ruck or rucksack: backpack issued to infantry in Vietnam.

S-1: Personnel staff officer.

S-2: Intelligence staff officer.

S-3: Operations staff officer.

Saddle up: The order to put on one's ruck and equipment to get ready to move out.

Sampan: a Vietnamese peasant's boat.

Sapper: a Việt Công or NVA commando, usually armed with explosives. Highly trained to infiltrate by stealth and employ explosives usually to breach a hole in the defensive perimeter or to blow up specific targets using satchel charges.

Satchel charges: pack used by the enemy containing explosives that is dropped or thrown and is generally more powerful than a grenade.

SF: Special Forces.

Shake'n bake: sergeant who attended NCO candidate (NCOC) school and earned rank after only a very short time in uniform.

Short: tour of duty being close to completion.

Short-timer: soldier nearing the end of his tour in Vietnam

Shrapnel: pieces of metal sent flying by an explosion.

SITREP: situation report.

Slick: a UH-1 helicopter used for transporting troops in tactical air assault operations. The helicopter did not have protruding armaments and was, therefore, "slick".

Smoke grenade: a grenade that released brightly colored smoke. Used for signaling.

Spider hole: camouflaged enemy foxhole.

Spooky: AC-47 is a propeller-driven aircraft with 3 Mini guns-capable of firing 6,000 rounds per minute per gun for a total of 18,000 rounds per minute.

SP pack or care package: cellophane packet containing toiletries and cigarettes which was sometimes given along with C-rations to soldiers in the field.

Stand to: Short for 'Stand-to-Arms'. At the process of stand-to each man would put on all combat gear and be prepared for an enemy attack since it was believed that most enemy attacks occurred immediately before dawn.

Stand-down: an infantry unit's return from the boonies to the base camp for refitting and training or to reduce alertness immediately following stand to.

Starlight scope: A night scope used to intensify images at night by using reflected light form the moon, stars or any other source of light.

Steel pot: the standard U.S. Army helmet. The steel pot was the outer metal cover. Often used to wash and shave with, heat water, and, sometimes, sit on.

Tanglefoot: single-strand barbed wire strung in a meshwork pattern at about ankle height. A barrier designed to make it difficult to cross the obstructed area by foot. Usually placed around defensive positions.

Thiu Úy: Vietnamese for Junior Lieutenant. U.S. Army Second Lieutenant equivalent.

TOC: tactical operations center.

Tracer: a round of ammunition chemically treated to glow or give off smoke so that its flight can be followed. M-16s used red tracers and AK-47s used green tracers.

Tracks: any vehicles which move on tracks rather than wheels.

Trip flare: a ground flare triggered by a trip wire used to signal and illuminate the approach of an enemy at night.

Trung Úy: Vietnamese for Lieutenant. U.S. Army First Lieutenant equivalent

Turtles: new replacements. They were called turtles because it took so long for them to arrive.

Two-niner-two: the RC-292 ground plane antenna which was used to extend the range of the MAT and the district team's PRC-25.

UH-1H: a Huey helicopter.

VC: Việt Cộng.

Victor Charlie: the Việt Cộng.

Việt Cộng: the Communist-led forces fighting the South Vietnamese government. The political wing was known as the National Liberation Front, and the military was called the People's Liberation Armed Forces.

Ville: Vietnamese hamlet or village.

VNAF: South Vietnamese Air Force.

White mice: South Vietnamese police. The nickname came from their uniform white helmets and gloves.

White phosphorus: a type of explosive round from artillery, mortars, or rockets. Also a type of aerial bomb. The rounds exploded with a huge puff of white smoke from the hotly burning phosphorus, and were used as marking rounds or incendiary rounds. When white phosphorus hit the skin it continued to burn. Water would not extinguish it. It had to be smothered or quickly cut out.

WIA: wounded in action.

Willy Peter: white phosphorus. Also called Willy Pete.

Woodline: a row of trees at the edge of a field or rice paddy.

WP: white phosphorus.

XO: executive officer; the second in command of a military unit.

BIBLIOGRAPHY

1st Battalion 12th Infantry Regiment, 4th Infantry Division
War Diary 1968–9. Fourth Division Association. 1 Aug.
2006.

After Action Report for A-244, Ben Het. 5th Special Forces
Group (Airborne), 1st Special Forces. APO San Francisco
96944: Detachment B-24, 1969.

Bonni McKeown. Peaceful Patriot, The Story of Tom Bennett.
First ed. Charleston, West Virginia: Mountain State Press,
1980.

Brigade Operations Staff, comp. United States Army. S-3 Section. Headquarters Second Brigade, Fourth Infantry Division. Daily Staff Journals (AR 220–346). Kontum, RVN,
1968–9.

Defense Plan for A-244, Ben Het. 5th Special Forces Group (Airborne), 1st Special Forces. APO San Francisco 96944: Detachment B-24, 1969.

Dilkes, Harry, and Lewis Easterly. Five Years to DEROS. New Brunswick, NJ: DPG Ltd. 2000.

Magazine, Infantry, ed. A Distant Challenge: The US Infantry-man in Vietnam 1967–70. First ed. Vol. 1. Birmingham, Alabama: Birmingham Company, 1971. 1–399.

Monthly Operational Summary (MOPSUM). Detachment A-244, 5th Special Forces Group (Airborne), 1st Special Forces, Camp Ben Het. APO San Francisco 96944: Detachment A-244, 31 Mar. 1969.

Neville, Daniel E., trans. "Battle of Dien Bien Phu." (2000). Nov.-Dec. 2005. <http://www.dienbienphu.org>

Prados, John. "The NVA's Operation Dien Bien Phu: The 1969 Siege of Ben Het." The VVA Veteran, the Vietnam Veterans of America, Incorporated (2003). 22 Sept. 2006. <http://theveteran@vva.org>

Schultries, Sergeant Ronald. "Red Warriors Give NVA Base Camp Housewarming." The Ivy Leaf, Jan. 1969.

Staff Journalist. "Kit Carson Scouts Flush Out VC." The Ivy Leaf, Jan.-Feb. 1969.

978-0-595-69931-5
0-595-69931-6

Printed in the United States
109525LV00004B/10-27/A